101
QUESTIONS

About Ellen White and Her Writings

William Fagal

Pacific Press® Publishing Association
Nampa, Idaho
Oshawa, Ontario, Canada
www.pacificpress.com

Cover design by Gerald Lee Monks
Cover design resources from the White Estate
Inside design by Aaron Troia

Copyright © 2010 by Pacific Press® Publishing Association
Printed in the United States of America

The author assumes full responsibility for the accuracy of all facts and quotations as cited in this book.

You can obtain additional copies of this book by calling toll-free 1-800-765-6955 or by visiting http://www.adventistbookcenter.com.

Scriptures quoted from NASB are from *The New American Standard Bible*®, Copyright © 1960, 1962, 1963, 1968, 1971, 1972, 1973, 1975, 1977, 1995 by The Lockman Foundation. Used by permission.

Scriptures quoted from KJV are from the King James Version.

Library of Congress Cataloging-in-Publication Data:

Fagal, William A.
  101 questions about Ellen White and her writings / William Fagal.
    p. cm.
  ISBN 13: 978-0-8163-2378-4 (pbk.)
  ISBN 10: 0-8163-2378-X (pbk.)
  1. White, Ellen Gould Harmon, 1827–1915—Miscellanea. 2. Seventh-day Adventists—
Doctrines—Miscellanea. I. Title.
  BX6193.W5F34 2010
  230'.6732—dc22

                                                                    2009043572

10 11 12 13 14 • 5 4 3 2 1

Dedication

This book is dedicated to my parents,

William A. Fagal (1919–1989) and Virginia M. Fagal (1917–),

who first introduced me to Ellen G. White's writings

and who were living examples to me of devotion, humility, and balance

in relation to the messages these writings contain.

Table of Contents

Preface

This book is made up of questions and answers. The questions are a sampling—though not necessarily a representative one—of those that people have sent to the Ellen G. White Estate (http://www.whiteestate.org) in recent years. With a couple of exceptions, the answers were written by William Fagal, an associate director of the White Estate. The names of those who submitted the questions don't appear on the Web site, and we haven't included them in this book either.

These questions and answers weren't written with publication in mind, so we've edited them for use in this book. The author has also modified several answers to reflect more recent thoughts and information or to meet the needs of readers. And to keep this book to a reasonable length, most of the answers published here have been abbreviated from those that appear on the Web site. Many of those answers contain entire documents or complete chapters of books.

You can read the full questions and answers on the White Estate Digital Resource Center Web site (http://drc.whiteestate.org). To help you find them, we've placed the Web site titles for the questions and answers in parentheses and quotation marks under the questions we use as "chapter" titles. Key the Web site titles into the search box in the upper left-hand corner of the Digital Resource Center Web page.

You may notice that in some instances, the Web site titles don't seem to fit the topics of the questions and answers that follow them. Often that's because the original inquiry contained multiple questions, and we've used a different question and answer than the one on which the Web site title was based.

We've followed the rather idiosyncratic form that has become customary in referencing quotations from Ellen White's books, periodical articles, and so forth. For the full bibliographic information on the works cited and the key to the abbreviations used, please see the bibliography at the back of this book.

May reading this book increase your understanding of and strengthen your faith in God's communication with us through His messengers, ancient and modern.

David C. Jarnes
Compiler/editor

Part 1

Questions About Ellen White and Her Inspiration

Question 1:

Was Ellen White a prophet like those who wrote the Bible?

("Was Ellen G. White a Prophet?")

My husband and I have had some vigorous arguments about Ellen White and her place in the church. He believes that she was a prophet and that her writings were just as inspired as the Bible. I believe she was inspired by God, just as I believe C. S. Lewis and other Christian writers were inspired by God to write what they did. However, I do not believe she was a prophet, and I do not think her writings were just as inspired as the Bible.

Is there any documented account of someone who was not an Adventist who approached Mrs. White with an open mind, devoid of preconceived bias either for or against her and became convinced by seeing her have visions or some other evidence that she was indeed a prophet?

All the books and materials I have ever seen about Mrs. White were published by the church and, therefore, are biased in her favor. It would be very easy for one to think that because the church makes a lucrative profit from selling her books that they naturally wish to promote her as a prophet.

If you are a C. S. Lewis fan (or even if you're not), you will probably appreciate this paragraph from his *Mere Christianity*. It is the last paragraph of his chapter "The Shocking Alternative":

> I am trying here to prevent anyone saying the really foolish thing that people often say about [Jesus]: "I'm ready to accept Jesus as a great moral teacher, but I don't accept His claim to be God." That is the one thing we must not say. A man who was merely a man and said the sort of things Jesus said would not be a great moral teacher. He would either be a lunatic—on a level with the man who says he is a poached egg—or else he would be the Devil of Hell. You must make your choice. Either this man was, and is, the Son of God: or else a madman or something worse. You can shut Him up for a fool, you can spit at Him and kill Him as a demon; or you can fall at His feet and call Him Lord and God. But let us not come with any patronizing nonsense about His being a great human teacher. He has not left that open to us. He did not intend to.

Isn't there a parallel to how we regard Mrs. White? It's on a much lower level, of course—she didn't claim to be God. But she did claim that her visions and her messages came from God by supernatural means (a claim C. S. Lewis never made about himself). If Mrs. White was wrong about that, what basis do we have for calling her inspired at all? Are there alternatives to concluding that she was who she said she was—a "messenger of the Lord"—or she was a lunatic or an agent of Satan?

If we had a documented account, you might find it convincing, even definitive. But I wouldn't recommend that you believe her claim on the strength of such an account. In fact, I think I would warn you against doing so. Why? Because the Bible doesn't say that the evidence of seeing a prophet in vision is a test of the genuineness of the gift. Further, experience has shown that such evidence may be counterfeited, either by evil people or by evil supernatural powers.

For example, after Mrs. White's death, a woman named Margaret Rowen claimed to be Ellen G. White's successor. People saw Margaret Rowen in "vision" and noted that she evidently did not breathe while in that state. This convinced a number of Adventists that she had the genuine gift. But she didn't. She forged a document naming her as Mrs. White's successor, which she claimed came from Mrs. White, and she lied about it to a doctor to get him to smuggle this document into Mrs. White's papers where it would be "found." She stole money that supporters sent to her office, and when the whole thing unraveled, she tried to kill the doctor when he turned against her. She ended up serving time in prison in California—but her visions had looked real!

The Bible gives us tests by which we are told to evaluate someone who claims to have the true prophetic gift.

1. A true prophet's predictions are fulfilled (see Deuteronomy 18:21, 22; Jeremiah 28:9). The Bible explicitly makes this a test for us to apply. But it also tells us that there are conditions, whether stated or implied, in some Bible prophecy. (See, for example, Jeremiah 18:7–10.)

2. A true prophet's messages harmonize with the Word of God (see Isaiah 8:20). Note the context—telling the true messenger from the false. So this is another Bible test.

3. A true prophet's ministry bears fitting fruit (see Matthew 7:15, 16). The Bible itself names one such fruit: that a prophet will give people God's message and turn them away from their sins. (See Jeremiah 23:22, and note the context preceding it.)

4. A true prophet tells the truth about Jesus' incarnation (see 1 John 4:1–3). The Bible says that a true prophet will acknowledge that Jesus' incarnation was real—that "the Word became flesh, and dwelt among us" (John 1:14, NASB).

I wonder if the "lucrative profit" motivation is all it is cracked up to be. A few years after Mrs. White's death, the trustees she had appointed in her will to look after her writings entered into an agreement with the General Conference. The agreement arranged for the church to support the work of the White Estate—the General Conference would underwrite the budget of the White Estate, and for its part, the White Estate would turn all royalties from Mrs. White's books into the General Conference treasury. This agreement is still in force. How is it working out? Well, the budget the church puts into the Ellen

G. White Estate is about six times the amount it receives in royalties from the books. It's pretty hard to find the profit motive there!

In my view, the church supports Mrs. White (including the White Estate) because it truly believes that her work was "a gift of light" that continues to shine on our path. Our experience has shown that when we have followed that gift of light, we have been blessed spiritually and our work has been effective. When, on the other hand, we have ignored that light and gone on our own, we have suffered loss.

We do not make Mrs. White another Bible writer—she herself ruled that out in such statements as this famous one: "Little heed is given to the Bible, and the Lord has given a lesser light to lead men and women to the greater light" (*Colporteur Ministry*, 125). But we do believe that the Lord used the same means of bringing light to her that He used with the Bible writers, and that He communicated with her more directly than He did with C. S. Lewis and other fine, insightful Christian writers.

Question 2:

Is *everything* Ellen White wrote inspired?

("Did Ellen G. White Say That Only Some of Her Writings Are Inspired? [1]")

> *Is it true that Ellen G. White says somewhere that only some of her writings are inspired from God? A friend of mine heard that she made the statement that only her testimonies are inspired.*

Here are a few statements that Mrs. White made about the authority of her writings:

> Many times in my experience I have been called upon to meet the attitude of a certain class, who acknowledged that the testimonies were from God, but took the position that this matter and that matter were Sister White's opinion and judgment. This suits those who do not love reproof and correction, and who, if their ideas are crossed, have occasion to explain the difference between the human and the divine.
>
> If the preconceived opinions or particular ideas of some are crossed in being reproved by testimonies, they have a burden at once to make plain their position to discriminate between the testimonies, defining what is Sister White's human judgment, and what is the word of the Lord. Everything that sustains their cherished ideas is divine, and the testimonies to correct their errors are human—Sister White's opinions. They make of none effect the counsel of God by their tradition (*Selected Messages*, 3:68 [Manuscript 16, 1889]).

> Sister White is not the originator of these books [those she wrote]. They contain the instruction that during her lifework God has been giving her. They contain the precious, comforting light that God has graciously given His servant to be given to the world (*Colporteur Ministry*, 125).

> I do not write one article in the paper expressing merely my own ideas. They are what God has opened before me in vision—the precious

rays of light shining from the throne (*Testimonies for the Church*, 5:67).

When the Holy Spirit reveals anything regarding the institutions connected with the Lord's work, or concerning the work of God upon human hearts and minds, as He has revealed these things through me in the past, the message given is to be regarded as light given of God for those who need it. But for one to mix the sacred with the common is a great mistake. . . .

There are times when common things must be stated, common thoughts must occupy the mind, common letters must be written and information given that has passed from one to another of the workers. Such words, such information, are not given under the special inspiration of the Spirit of God (*Selected Messages*, 1:38, 39).

Question 3:
Are Ellen White's writings a "lesser light"?
("Lesser Light, Greater Light")

> *I have heard many people say that the writings of Mrs. White are a lesser light compared to the Bible. They usually quote a statement she made that's in the* Review and Herald, *January 20, 1903 (also* Selected Messages, *3:30).*
>
> *However, in that statement she does not explicitly say the Bible is a greater light and the* Testimonies *are a lesser light. The first paragraph states that her books are to lead men and women to the Savior. She says that people have neglected the Bible, the mission of which is to point people to Christ, and God has sent a lesser light to lead men and women to the greater light, which should be Christ according to the context of the statement. In that letter she was not discussing the relationship between her writing and the Bible. The context is about the light that needs to reach the people by the* Testimonies. *I believe that if the Bible was written by people who were inspired and E. G. White was inspired, then they're on the same level, since it is the Holy Spirit who inspires.*

What you say about the paragraph just before the often-quoted one is true: Mrs. White does say that her books are to lead people to the Savior. But neither in that paragraph nor even in the whole document does she identify Jesus as the "greater light." You will notice that in the paragraph we are discussing she describes the lesser-light writings in theological terms, "carry out the principles they contain" and "rejoicing in the light of present truth," rather than in personal terms, such as "come to know the Savior" or "give one's heart to the Lord." If her point were that the greater light is Jesus, and the lesser light was to bring people to Him, wouldn't we expect her to develop this personal side of the matter as she enlarged on her statement? But instead, she develops her statement along the lines of principles and truth, such as we would associate with the Bible.

Here is the full paragraph:

The Lord has sent His people much instruction, line upon line, precept upon precept, here a little, and there a little. Little heed is given to the Bible, and the Lord has given a lesser light to lead men and women to the greater light. Oh, how much good would be accomplished if the books containing this light were read with a determination to carry out the principles they contain! There would be a thousandfold greater vigilance, a thousandfold more self-denial and resolute effort. And many more would now be rejoicing in the light of present truth.

In context, the paragraph above is clearly talking about her own books as providing "much instruction" that "the Lord has sent His people" and as "containing this light"—an expression she used in the very next sentence after the famous quote about the lesser and greater light. The natural way to understand her reference here, it seems to me, is the way we have always done so: lesser light—the contents of her writings; greater light—the Bible.

This conclusion is strengthened, I think, by noting another place where Mrs. White explicitly spoke of the relationship between her writings and the Bible: *Testimonies for the Church,* volume 5, pages 663–665.

Brother J would confuse the mind by seeking to make it appear that the light God has given through the *Testimonies* is an addition to the word of God, but in this he presents the matter in a false light. God has seen fit in this manner to bring the minds of His people to His word, to give them a clearer understanding of it. . . .

It is because you have neglected to acquaint yourselves with God's inspired Book that He has sought to reach you by simple, direct testimonies, calling your attention to the words of inspiration which you had neglected to obey, and urging you to fashion your lives in accordance with its pure and elevated teachings.

The Lord designs to warn you, to reprove, to counsel, through the testimonies given, and to impress your minds with the importance of the truth of His word. The written testimonies are not to give new light, but to impress vividly upon the heart the truths of inspiration already revealed.

There are important parallels between these two statements, the famous one you asked about and this one. Both refer explicitly to the Bible and to Mrs. White's writings. Both make the point that Mrs. White's books will help a person see the light. And in this second reference, it is clear that Mrs. White's writings direct people's attention to Scripture.

Question 4:
Did God give Ellen White the very words He wanted her to write?
("Verbal Inspiration")

Do you have a compilation that knocks the idea of verbal inspiration?

I don't know of a compilation that does this, but the primary statement from Mrs. White that addresses this question is her description of how inspiration worked in her own experience. This is from the *Review and Herald* of October 8, 1867; it comes in the midst of a discussion of healthful dress for women:

> A third class passed before me with cheerful countenances, and free, elastic step. Their dress was the length I have described as proper, modest and healthful. It cleared the filth of the street and side-walk a few inches under all circumstances, such as ascending and descending steps, et cetera.
>
> As I have before stated, the length was not given me in inches, and I was not shown a lady's boot. And here I would state that although I am as dependent upon the Spirit of the Lord in writing my views as I am in receiving them, yet the words I employ in describing what I have seen are my own, unless they be those spoken to me by an angel, which I always enclose in marks of quotation. As I wrote upon the subject of dress the view of those three companies revived in my mind as plain as when I was viewing them in vision; but I was left to describe the length of the proper dress in my own language the best I could, which I have done by stating that the bottom of the dress should reach near the top of a lady's boot, which would be necessary in order to clear the filth of the streets under the circumstances before named.

To get a feel for the whole discussion and what prompted this response, read the paragraphs that precede this one.

Two places where Mrs. White discusses inspiration as a topic are *Selected Messages,* book 1, in the first forty pages or so, and in the introduction to *The*

Great Controversy. Paying close attention to what she was saying in these passages will go a long way toward giving us a better concept of inspiration than the verbal one.

Question 5:
Did Ellen White make mistakes?
("Mistakes of Ellen G. White")

> *I was a Web site defending the work of Ellen White. There is one thing that is a bit surprising to me. It says, "Ellen White did make mistakes." How many mistakes did she make, and how can I be sure what part of her work is true and what part is mistaken? She said some things—many things—that seem like mistakes, and I would like to know if they just seem to be mistakes or they really are—for example, what she said about novels, theater, wedding rings, sports like tennis, etc.*

The question you are really asking is, Did Ellen G. White give mistaken instruction for the church—instruction that reflects only her human perceptions rather than the divine will? You offer several examples of things that to some seem like mistakes. I notice that they all have to do with matters of lifestyle.

We are all subject to a very human tendency, which is to defend as right whatever we want to do. When someone comes along and says that what we're doing isn't right, we instinctively conclude that he or she is wrong or mistaken. Mrs. White saw this happen many times in her ministry. She wrote,

> If the preconceived opinions or particular ideas of some are crossed in being reproved by testimonies, they have a burden at once to make plain their position to discriminate between the testimonies, defining what is Sister White's human judgment, and what is the word of the Lord. Everything that sustains their cherished ideas is divine, and the testimonies to correct their errors are human—Sister White's opinions. They make of none effect the counsel of God by their tradition. —Manuscript 16, 1889 (*Selected Messages,* 3:68).

On the homepage of the site that you referred to, one of the main links says, "Ellen White Did Make Mistakes." When you click there, you see a brief essay on the question. Notice what the first paragraph says about the mistakes it is referring to.

Ellen White herself never claimed that it was impossible for her to err when it came to historical details, dates, and other such information. She made it clear that neither she, nor Bible prophets were God's "pen" but were rather His "penmen." Some of the chronological discrepancies in the Bible (so often pointed out by Bible critics) are good examples of what she meant ("Ellen White Did Make Mistakes," http://www.ellen-white.com/EllenWhiteMistakes.html).

So these are the kinds of mistakes the Web site is referring to—things like details of history, dates, etc. On one occasion, Mrs. White mentioned something about forty rooms in the Paradise Valley Sanitarium. One man seized on this to say that it had made him lose all confidence in Mrs. White because he knew for a fact that there were only thirty-eight rooms in the sanitarium. She chided him for putting common matters on the same level as the spiritual (see *Selected Messages,* book 1, pages 38, 39). Mrs. White claimed no inspiration regarding common matters. But on matters of spiritual instruction for the church, she understood that she was to give the instruction that the Lord had given her, not what was merely her own opinion.

Sometimes conditions change, and with them, the application of the instruction she gave. For instance, at one point in the nineteenth century, Mrs. White came out strongly against Seventh-day Adventists purchasing bicycles. Today, most Seventh-day Adventists have bicycles or had them as children. Was Mrs. White's counsel a mistake? No. She protested large expenditures of funds for bicycles (which, at the time she wrote, typically cost an amount equal to many months of earnings) with no more purpose than to display one's "toy" or to compete in races. While some bicycles might still fit in that category, most are of modest cost and provide healthful recreation and transportation. The conditions have changed, and so the application of the counsel has changed. The counsel she gave regarding bicycles might apply just as well to some other extravagant expenditures today.

In regard to the examples you have asked about, you might take a careful look to see if you can discover the principles that drove the specifics of her counsel. Have conditions changed in such a way as to affect how the principles might be applied? For instance, to take just one item that you mentioned,

Mrs. White objected to the theater principally because of its moral content. Has the theater (or today, the movies and even television programming) improved to the point where Christians may go and find that they are drawn closer to the Lord as a result? Will the experience better fit them for heaven or for being channels the Holy Spirit can use to win souls to the Savior? Or does the theater tend to revel in the very sins that put our Lord on the cross? Looking at the principles that underlie her counsels, we might well ask, Is the theater where Christians should seek entertainment?

I think that if you will look for the principles that provided the basis for the counsel you have asked about, you will find that the counsel was not mistaken when it was given and that in general the counsel still applies very well. Saying this does not imply that the counsel will be popular, for we all have the tendency I wrote of at the beginning of this message—the tendency to justify what our fallen natures tell us will be interesting, fun, or desirable and is widely practiced by others. But as Christians, we are not called to follow the crowd nor to follow the promptings of our own desires. Jesus said, "Be thou faithful unto death, and I will give thee a crown of life" (Revelation 2:10, KJV).

Question 6:
Were Ellen White's visions the result of epilepsy?
("Ellen G. White's Visions a Result of Epilepsy?")

> *I happened onto a Web site listed in my search results while I was look-*
> *ing up the Ellen G. White Estate site, and I became engrossed in reading*
> *the material presented because of its credible, nonattacking style. The in-*
> *formation was regarding Ellen White's visions. Basically, the site strongly*
> *suggested the visions were linked to what is called temporal lobe epilepsy*
> *with hypergraphia resulting from brain damage that could have resulted*
> *from the rock-throwing incident when Ellen White was a young girl. I*
> *have to confess their evidence is quite compelling and discomforting.*

Style can be as deceptive as content. One should be careful about granting credibility to someone because of style before ascertaining all the facts involved.

There was a doctor or two who made these claims in the 1980s; I don't remember their names now. Neither was a specialist in temporal lobe epilepsy, the condition they concluded was the cause of her visions. At Loma Linda University, Dr. Donald I. Peterson, a professor of neurology (the appropriate specialty) and chief of neurology at Riverside General Hospital, convened a panel of qualified specialists, Adventist and non-Adventist, to look at the evidence. They concluded that her experience did not match that of people suffering from temporal lobe epilepsy. Apparently, science is on Mrs. White's side on this one.

Dr. Peterson wrote a brief little booklet on the matter, "Visions or Seizures: Was Ellen White the Victim of Epilepsy?" It is now out of print but is available on the Ellen G. White Estate Web site.

Question 7:
Did Ellen White plagiarize other people's books?
("Did Ellen G. White Plagiarized Some of Her Writings?")

It has been brought to my attention that Ellen G. White allegedly plagiarized in producing some of her writings. Please tell me who made these charges, when this plagiarism supposedly occurred, in what book or books, what portion of those books allegedly contain copying, and any other circumstance involving plagiarism.

Around 1980 or so, an Adventist minister by the name of Walter Rea began to make serious charges against Ellen G. White to the effect that she got her messages out of books by other authors rather than from the Lord and that her writings were merely plagiarisms from the writings of others passed off as her own.[1] Rea wrote a book expounding his charges with considerable bombast. Church publications such as the *Adventist Review* and *Ministry* carried articles relating to these matters through a good part of the 1980s. In addition, as you might expect, the Ellen G. White Estate prepared documents about these things.

Did Ellen White ever use the wording of someone else in her writings without giving credit? Yes, she did. Here at the office we have a set of her books in which we have marked all the passages that the critics or our own staff and others have found that bear a clear resemblance to passages in other works that she had access to. Walter Rea once claimed that 90 percent of her work was copied. This is both an overstatement and a misrepresentation. No objective measure of this phenomenon comes anywhere near that amount.

The General Conference asked Dr. Fred Veltman, then chairman of the religion department at Pacific Union College, to undertake a study of the book *The Desire of Ages* to ascertain how much literary relationship it might hold to previously published books. Dr. Veltman chose fifteen chapters randomly in order to keep the study manageable. Even so, it took him and a few helpers several years to do the job.

Dr. Veltman drew up about seven classifications of possible relationship,

---

1. Ed.: Not the first such charge, but one that raised the issue for current generations.

from the very remote to a word-for-word parallel. I don't recall that he found any of the latter, but he did find close paraphrases and other looser correspondences. The looser they are, the more debatable they may be, but for the sake of completeness, he included them. He came up with a figure of around 30 percent of the material he studied that resembled, to a greater or lesser degree, the works of others that Ellen G. White may have consulted. Where the correspondence is fairly close, I don't think there is any doubt that Mrs. White utilized the other work. Where it is not so close, borrowing would be more difficult to prove. On those, I am more willing to reserve judgment.

What does this all mean? Was Mrs. White a fraud, attempting to deceive people by passing off the works of others as her own? No, I don't believe so. In the *Review and Herald* and in *Signs of the Times,* she recommended *The Life and Epistles of St. Paul,* by Conybeare and Howson—a book she was drawing on for her own book *Sketches From the Life of Paul,* which would be published the following year. This is not the behavior of someone attempting to hide a dishonest practice. Further, she openly proclaimed in the introduction to *The Great Controversy* that she had used the writings of others, sometimes without giving credit. She also says why. Here is the statement from pages xi and xii:

> The great events which have marked the progress of reform in past ages are matters of history, well known and universally acknowledged by the Protestant world; they are facts which none can gainsay. This history I have presented briefly, in accordance with the scope of the book, and the brevity which must necessarily be observed, the facts having been condensed into as little space as seemed consistent with a proper understanding of their application. In some cases where a historian has so grouped together events as to afford, in brief, a comprehensive view of the subject, or has summarized details in a convenient manner, his words have been quoted; but in some instances no specific credit has been given, since the quotations are not given for the purpose of citing that writer as authority, but because his statement affords a *ready* and *forcible presentation* of the subject. In narrating the experience and views of those carrying forward the work of reform in our own time, similar use has been made of their published works (emphasis added).

Mrs. White's concern was to get the meaning across. If others had expressed well the meaning that she wanted to convey, she felt free to use their words without credit if she was not citing the other author as an authority. Was this legitimate? Several Adventist scholars who have done substantial, careful reading in nineteenth-century Bible commentators came to the conclusion that this was common practice in Ellen White's day and before; the commentators borrowed heavily from one another and almost never gave credit. (For example, Fred Veltman in a *Ministry* magazine article reported on his findings in the study of *The Desire of Ages*.)

Before Mrs. White's time, John Wesley followed the same practice. I have a statement of his in which he says that when he began to write and preach, he determined that he would note the source of every idea he drew from someone else. But then he said he finally decided to note none of them because it distracted from the point that he wanted to make and he couldn't always be sure he had properly given the source for every such item. Mrs. White grew up in the Methodist tradition; perhaps this view of Wesley's was something she adopted early on.

In any event, we can say that Mrs. White's practice was not inconsistent with the standards of her day, and she acknowledged her practice and the reasons for it in the introduction to *The Great Controversy*.

Was it plagiarism? The General Conference legal department hired a lawyer who specializes in copyright issues to review Mrs. White's writings and the charges that were being brought against her. After the lawyer spent three hundred hours at this task, he said there is no case. Ramik said that he would be delighted to defend Mrs. White in a court of law on these issues (not that any such case was going to be brought) because he felt he could win hands down. (See "There Simply Is No Case," *Adventist Review*, September 17, 1981, 6. This article is an interview by the *Adventist Review* staff of attorney Vincent Ramik, senior partner of Diller, Ramik, & Wight, Ltd., specialists in patent, trademark, and copyright cases, Washington, D.C. The article and three others on the same topic have been reprinted in a pamphlet—"Was Ellen G. White a Plagiarist?"—available from the Ellen G. White Estate.)

Question 8:
Did Ellen White's literary assistants write her books?
("Ellen G. White's Visions a Result of Epilepsy?")

> *On a Web site, I read an article about a Fannie Bolton, whom Ellen G. White is reported to have hired and fired several times—four, I think. This article was a bit discomforting in that it pointed out several major inconsistencies between what Mrs. White wrote to others and what she practiced herself. It also made the assertion that she actually did not do a good share of the writing; her assistants did.*

I don't know the specific point made in the article you refer to concerning her handling of Fannie Bolton. If you are interested, you may wish to obtain a copy of *The Fannie Bolton Story,* a collection of all the known letters of Ellen White, Fannie Bolton, and their associates that have a bearing on these matters. (You can access *The Fanny Bolton Story* on the White Estate Digital Resource Center Web site.)

I can help you more directly with the question of whether Mrs. White or her literary helpers wrote her materials. On our Web site, www.WhiteEstate .org, in the section "Issues & Answers," you will find a subsection titled "Questions and Answers About Ellen G. White." It contains the material that follows:

> What were Ellen White's secretaries and literary assistants permitted to do in regard to her writings?
>
> Ellen White did not always use perfect grammar, spelling, punctuation, or sentence or paragraph construction in her writing. She freely acknowledged her lack of such technical skills. In 1873 she lamented, "I am not a scholar. I cannot prepare my own writings for the press. . . . I am not a grammarian" (*Selected Messages,* book 3, p. 90). She felt the need of help from others in the preparation of her manuscripts for publication. W. C. White describes the boundaries that his mother set for her workers:
>
> > "Mother's copyists are entrusted with the work of correcting grammatical errors, of eliminating unnecessary repetitions, and of

grouping paragraphs and sections in their best order. . . .

"Mother's workers of experience, such as Sisters Davis, Burn-
ham, Bolton, Peck, and Hare, who are very familiar with her writings, are authorized to take a sentence, paragraph, or section from
one manuscript and incorporate it with another manuscript where
the same thought was expressed but not so clearly. But none of
Mother's workers are authorized to add to the manuscripts by
introducing thoughts of their own" (W. C. White to G. A. Irwin,
May 7, 1900).

While the chapters for each book were being prepared, Ellen White
was constantly consulted, and when the work was completed, it was
given to her for final approval.

At the age of 75 she explained her work to her sister, Mary:

"Now, my sister, do not think that I have forgotten you; for I
have not. You know that I have books to make. My last effort is a
book on true education. The writing of this book has been very trying to me, but it is nearly finished. I am now completing the last
chapter. This book will not have in it so much matter as there is in
some of my larger works, but the instruction it contains is important. I feel the need of help from God continually.

"I am still as active as ever. I am not in the least decrepit. I am
able to do much work, writing and speaking as I did years ago.

"I read over all that is copied, to see that everything is as it
should be. I read all the book manuscript before it is sent to the
printer. So you can see that my time must be fully occupied" (Letter 133, 1902).

There is ample testimony from Mrs. White's secretaries—not only in public statements but in private correspondence with the publishers, etc.—that
they worked only on what she had written; they did not write material for
her.

Fannie Bolton made public retractions of her claims that she had written
Mrs. White's materials. You will find these included in the document I men-

tioned to you. Later, after both Fannie Bolton and Mrs. White were dead, a critic of Mrs. White claimed that he had irrefutable proof that Fannie, not Mrs. White, had written *Steps to Christ.* But he never set forth such proof. In fact, the claim was nonsense because one can find portions of *Steps to Christ* in material Mrs. White wrote and published before she ever met Fannie Bolton. (*Steps to Christ,* like many of Mrs. White's later books, was drawn from her earlier writings, both published and unpublished, which were organized into the book we now know.) So the proof is there that this was Mrs. White's material, not Fannie's.

See also the following question and answer.

Question 9:
Did Ellen White's secretary write *Steps to Christ*?
("*Steps to Christ* Written by Ellen G. White?")

Someone wrote me and said that Steps to Christ *was not written by Ellen G. White but by a secretary and that there are no original manuscripts for that book. Is this true?*

It is true that there is not an original manuscript for *Steps to Christ*. There are two reasons for this:

1. Mrs. White typically did not keep the working papers for the things she had written after they had appeared in print. This was a matter of practicality.

2. Especially in the latter half of her life, she did not write out her book manuscripts as new compositions. Rather, she and her staff would plan an outline for a book, and the staff would locate things she had written previously, whether published or in her letters and manuscripts, which contributed to the thoughts they wished to develop. The staff assembled these, and if needed, Mrs. White would write additional material to fill in the gaps or improve the flow. When she was satisfied with the book, it went to press. In such circumstances, one would not expect to find a "manuscript" for the book.

Did Ellen White's secretary write *Steps to Christ*? No. The method of composing the book that I have described above would lead us to expect to find portions of it in Mrs. White's earlier writings. And, indeed, we do. In the 1930s, when the charge you read first surfaced, D. E. Robinson wrote a response in which he listed a number of parts of *Steps to Christ* that were drawn from articles by Mrs. White that had been published earlier. He also told more about the source of the charge and the secretary who the critic claimed was the author. You can access what he wrote in the Digital Resource Center on the Ellen G. White Web site. It's the second half of a document titled "The Story of a Popular Book 'Steps to Christ' and The Authorship of 'Steps to Christ.' "

Question 10:
Did Ellen White say she spoke with her dead husband in a vision?
("The Dream of Dead Husband")

> *I have seen a lot of anti-Ellen White documents on the Internet. I do not give any credence to most, but one thing that struck me was an allegation that she spoke with her dead husband in a vision. I know there must be an explanation for this, but I can't think of one. Could you please help me with this?*

The account of this dream of Mrs. White's is published in two places: *The Retirement Years,* pages 161–163, and *Manuscript Releases,* volume 10, pages 38–40. This account is not a revelation by one of Mrs. White's critics of previously hidden and damning evidence about her. Rather, it is an account of an interesting and completely understandable incident from Ellen White's life that the White Estate trustees felt might be of interest to people who had also lost their life companions.

In the dream, James seemed to have come back to life, and thus, Mrs. White expresses the natural wish that they might continue on together. In reality, though, she knew that it was just a dream—that's what she calls it—though one with a message from God in answer to her prayer. Mrs. White's critics wish to portray it as a kind of spiritualist communing with the dead. It was no such thing. The dream was vivid and seemed real, as dreams often do. But in Mrs. White's waking reflections, she never imagined that she had actually been talking with James or with his "spirit." In the dream, she even puts it this way: "Father, I saw you die; I saw you buried. Has the Lord pitied me and let you come back to me again, and we work together as we used to?" This indicates her belief in resurrection, not spiritualism, or else they could not work together as they "used to."

It seems to me that people who are not looking for some basis on which to criticize Mrs. White will read her account as an appealing human-interest story of a grieving prophet. In this instance, the Lord communicated with her in a dream—in a manner that was sure to command her attention. She herself did not think the dream meant that James had actually appeared to her in any real way. Why should we take it otherwise?

The Bible records a dream in which Joseph saw the sheaves of his brothers bow down to his sheaf. Where did the dream come from? Wouldn't we say it was from God even though it showed things that we would consider devilish if they happened in real life? In the dream, they had meaning, and they were portrayed to convey that meaning. So it is with Mrs. White's dream.

Question 11:

Why do Ellen and James White have an obelisk on their graves?

("Obelisk on Ellen G. White's Grave?")

> *I have been told that Ellen White and her husband each have an obelisk over their graves. Is this true, and if it is, could you tell me the history of it?*

Some people have expressed surprise and concern to find a monument in the shape of an obelisk on the family cemetery plot of James and Ellen White. The obelisk (one, not two) isn't a tombstone for any one person buried there but rather serves as the family marker in the center of the plot. The concern arises because of the obelisk's connection to pagan worship in Egypt and to other questionable associations. Evidently, however, many people in the nineteenth century didn't think this was a problem. Obelisks were common markers in cemeteries of the day. Within sight of the White family plot there may be as many as twenty or thirty other grave or plot markers in the form of an obelisk. A similar situation exists at the cemetery in Rochester, New York, where some of Adventism's early pioneers were laid to rest. It's quite unlikely that all these people were Freemasons, nor were they adherents of ancient sun-worship religions. Use of the obelisk for a marker in a cemetery was simply a common occurrence, not a tribute to Masonic or pagan beliefs. Adventists of that era seem to be among the ones who saw no problem with the use of an obelisk.

We recently found correspondence relating to this question among the letters of George I. Butler, who was General Conference president when James White died in 1881 and for a number of years after. On February 12, 1884, Elder Butler wrote to Mrs. White: "The dark colored granite monument at B.C. [Battle Creek] which you looked at I ordered for your husband's grave last week at your son Willie's invitation. He told me to have it charged to you."

This indicates that Mrs. White had seen the monument chosen, and probably W. C. White had seen it too. W. C. White gave Elder Butler approval for its purchase. A letter from Elder Butler to W. C. White on February 10 of that year discussed the cost of the monument "with the headstone and other stones" and said that it "will be erected as soon as you send on the inscription." It is clear that the White family was involved in the selection of the monument.

Twenty years later, in 1904, Mrs. White wrote about a different suggestion for James White's monument: "After my husband had been laid away in the grave, his friends thought of putting up a broken shaft as a monument. 'Never!' said I, 'never! He has done, singlehanded, the work of three men. Never shall a broken monument be placed over his grave!' " (*Selected Messages,* 1:105). We can only guess, but it may be that in contrast to that suggestion, she was quite pleased to have such a well-formed, symmetrical monument placed on the family plot.

Some have asked about the supposed connection of the obelisk to Freemasonry. Seeing the obelisk on the family plot, a few have even supposed that Mrs. White herself must have been involved in the Masonic movement. This is an unwarranted conclusion. Mrs. White was an outspoken opponent of Freemasonry. While she was in Australia, she urged an Adventist worker who was deeply entangled in Freemasonry to sever his connection with it. She also counseled others against involvement with Masonic orders. (See *Evangelism,* 617–623; *Selected Messages,* 2:120–140.)

So why the obelisk on the White family cemetery plot? Evidently, Mrs. White didn't regard it as inherently a Masonic or pagan symbol, regardless of the fact—whether known to her or not—that Masons and sun worshipers had used it that way. Symbols mean what people take them to mean. The cross itself was once an abhorrent symbol of Roman oppression and cruelty, but today, Christians around the world hold it as a symbol of our redemption through Christ.

Symbols may change their meaning. When James White began to publish the *Advent Review and Sabbath Herald* as a biweekly paper (it became weekly in September of 1853), each issue carried both the date of publication and the standard name for the day of the week on which it was published, whether Monday or Thursday. (The day of publication varied some at that time.) Soon, however, he made a change. The issue published "Thursday, May 12, 1853," was followed two weeks later by one bearing the date of publication "Fifth-day, May 26, 1853." For several decades after that, the paper designated its publication day variously as "Fifth-day" and "Third-day" (for Tuesday)— apparently out of concern over the days of the week having been named for pagan gods. By the January 1, 1880, issue, however, the paper returned to using the standard names of the days of the week. Apparently our pioneers decided that the use of those names didn't compromise their faith.

People who use the standard names of the days of the week today don't do so to express devotion to pagan gods. The names simply don't symbolize those gods anymore, regardless of what they may have meant originally. Similarly, while obelisks may once have communicated occult meaning, by the nineteenth century, this meaning was no longer significant for most people other than Freemasons. Clearly, Mrs. White didn't hold such beliefs herself. (This answer has been modified substantially from the one that was originally used on the Web site in answer to the question above.)

Question 12:
Did Ellen White's 1856 prophecy fail?
("1856 Prophecy")

> *I joined the Seventh-day Adventist Church a while ago and am satis-*
> *fied with many of its doctrines, yet I'm very critical of Ellen G. White. I*
> *do not believe that she was a prophet, but I'm willing to keep an open*
> *mind. Perhaps the largest stumbling block is the failed 1856 prophecy of*
> *Christ's return in the lifetimes of people living then. Ellen White said that*
> *an angel told her that this was the case. This was allegedly direct heavenly*
> *revelation.*
>
> *I read your apologetic on this issue of it being a conditional prophecy.*
> *I'm fully aware of the conditional nature of some prophecy, and it cer-*
> *tainly makes sense. But what was conditional about this prophecy? Was it*
> *practical that the gospel would have been preached around the whole*
> *world in her time? In other words, what exactly were the failings of the*
> *church? That would have been a pretty quick missionary trip around the*
> *world for only fifty years or however long people who were at that confer-*
> *ence lived after it.*

Jonah's message, "Yet forty days, and Nineveh shall be overthrown" (Jonah 3:4, KJV), was a direct heavenly revelation too. I haven't yet seen any hint in Scripture that Jonah was given more of a message than this. The Ninevites merely hoped that God might have mercy on them if they repented—it was not a part of Jonah's message. This is clear from Jonah 3:9. But even though the message had been given with no ifs, ands, or buts, God did change the outcome based on what the people did (verse 10). The principle of condition-ality in prophecy is explicit in Jeremiah 18:7–10.

I do understand the condition to have been the carrying of God's last warn-ing messages to the world. I confess that in practical terms the task looks im-possible. But in matters like these we are dealing with more than the human. When we human beings give ourselves to cooperate fully with God, respond-ing to His leading and making Him first, He can do marvelous things with us, in us, and through us.

The church's failure to carry the Lord's message to the world was the result of something rooted in people's relationship to God. In *Testimonies for the Church,* volume 1, on the same page as the statement you asked about, there is a hint of where a problem might lie that would prevent the carrying out of God's purpose:

> Many dress like the world, to have an influence. But here they make a sad and fatal mistake. If they would have a true and saving influence, let them live out their profession, show their faith by their righteous works, and make the distinction great between the Christian and the world. I saw that the words, the dress, and actions should tell for God. Then a holy influence will be shed upon all, and all will take knowledge of them that they have been with Jesus. Unbelievers will see that the truth we profess has a holy influence and that faith in Christ's coming affects the character of the man or woman. If any wish to have their influence tell in favor of the truth, let them live it out and thus imitate the humble Pattern (*Testimonies for the Church,* 1:132).

Though Mrs. White mentions dress in the paragraph above, I take it that this was merely indicative of the underlying problem—hearts not fully given to God. Later in 1856, Mrs. White was given a vision that was shocking to the Adventist people—that it was they, not just the non-Sabbath keeping Adventists, who were "Laodicea" in Revelation 3 (see *Testimonies,* 1:141).

So the underlying problem of the church was a lack of full commitment to God. People's hearts were still set on the world and the things of the world. We need to get the heart right, then the actions will also be right, and God will be able to use us to finish His work. Even today, when we have such marvelous communication and travel tools, the task is greater than what we can handle. It will only be accomplished by people who are totally committed to God and to His service. He then will use means beyond our imagining to make our efforts fruitful to accomplish His tasks. It will be exciting to see what God does with people when they hold nothing back from Him!

See also the question and answer titled "Food for Worms" on the White Estate Web site.

Question 13:

Did Ellen White contradict Scripture regarding the "day and hour"?

("Day and Hour Revealed?")

> *I am curious about Ellen G. White's statement in her first vision that the Advent people hear the voice of God revealing to them the day and the hour of Christ's coming. Is she saying that the last-day saints will receive the knowledge of the actual day and hour of the Second Coming? How can we square this with the plain statements of Scripture indicating the contrary? And how can this vision be harmonized with her own later statements on time setting?*

Regarding your first question, I do understand Mrs. White's statement to mean that the last-day saints will receive the knowledge of the actual day and hour of the Second Coming. You asked how we can square this with the plain statements of Scripture indicating the contrary. I suppose you have in mind Matthew 24:36; 25:13; and Mark 13:32. All of these verses use the present tense to say that no one knows. None of them uses the future tense to say that no one will ever know. At the time Jesus spoke the words, they were certainly true. And I believe that they remain true for the human family, certainly through probationary time. But this does not rule out a change of condition before Jesus comes.

I suspect that at least one aspect of His quoted statements has already changed, though I can't prove it. Mark 13:32 says not only that no man knows the day or hour of His coming, but also that neither the angels nor Jesus Himself knows it. While that was true when it was spoken, is it still true that Jesus doesn't know when He will return? I can't prove it, but I suspect that at this point He does know. Certainly at some point before He leaves the heavenly courts to appear in the clouds of the sky He will know. So we must be careful not to make absolute what Scripture does not.

Regarding your second question, Mrs. White's warnings against time setting are always in the context of probationary time. That is, people arise claiming to know when Jesus will return and urging people to repent and be ready. Mrs. White was shown that our message is never again to be based on such predictions. But the instance you asked about, which Mrs. White was shown in the first vision, takes place very shortly before Jesus returns. (See *Early Writings,* 15.) It is after the close of probation. At that stage in salvation history, there is no longer any labor for sinners; the evangelistic work of God's people is done. Mrs. White's vision didn't portray them as taking the news of the time to others. Rather, God simply reveals to His people the time of their deliverance when it is very near, perhaps only days or hours away. It is not a message that they are given to proclaim to the world, for it is too late for that.

So in light of the fact that the Bible does not rule out a future revelation of the time, if God should choose to reveal to His faithful people—at the height of their trauma of being persecuted and hunted—just how near their deliverance is, why should this be a problem? Can't He do that? This is how I personally view the matter.

Question 14:
Did Ellen White mistakenly confuse two Herods?
("Seeming Contradictions Between 1SG 71 and 3SP 334")

I have seen a supposed mistake by Ellen White that I don't understand. Someone claims that she mistakenly spoke of two Herods as one. The two statements that are contrasted are Spiritual Gifts, *1:71, and* The Spirit of Prophecy, *3:334, the first one being said to be a mistake. Please clarify this for me.*

Yes, the two statements differ. The latter one is the more accurate in that it does not portray the Herod who killed John the Baptist and presided at the trial of Jesus as the same one who killed James and tried to kill Peter. Some have concluded that Mrs. White changed this matter in her later volume to try to cover up her "error." But this overlooks the fact that volume 1 of *Spiritual Gifts* was reproduced completely in *Early Writings,* which was published in 1882, four years after volume 3 of *The Spirit of Prophecy* was published—and the original statement can still be found in *Early Writings,* pages 185, 186. (In later printings, a note has been added that acknowledges the two Herods and offers an explanation—not a very strong one in my opinion.)

To me, the source of the confusion is clear—it is Scripture itself that calls them both Herod, and Ellen White was simply following Scripture in this. She wrote later, "I take the Bible just as it is, as the Inspired Word. I believe its utterances in an entire Bible" (*Selected Messages,* 1:17). I am not troubled by the fact that at this early stage (1858) she did not know every aspect of Bible-related history. (Nor did she know it all later, either.) It seems to me that when she had additional information on this point, she did the responsible thing— she used the better information in her next presentation of this part of the Bible's story.

Those who accuse her on this matter are assuming a view of inspiration in which there can be no human error. Seventh-day Adventists at large do not subscribe to that view. Mrs. White did not claim such a thing for herself. She wrote, "In regard to infallibility, I never claimed it; God alone is infallible. His word is true, and in Him is no variableness, or shadow of turning" (ibid., 37).

Question 15:
Did an Ellen White vision picture people on Saturn?
("Ellen G. White and Jupiter")

Recently, someone asked me about a vision in which Ellen White saw Jupiter and Saturn. It was claimed that there is a letter by a Mrs. Truesdail that says Mrs. White said she saw inhabitants there enjoying a meal. Do you know anything about this claim and the veracity of the letter?

There is a letter from Mrs. Truesdail, quoted by J. N. Loughborough in his *The Great Second Advent Movement,* pages 260, 261. I assume that this is the letter you are referring to. Here is what Loughborough quotes,

"Sister White was in very feeble health, and while prayers were offered in her behalf, the Spirit of God rested upon us. We soon noticed that she was insensible to earthly things. This was her first view of the planetary world. After counting aloud the moons of Jupiter, and soon after those of Saturn, she gave a beautiful description of the rings of the latter. She then said, 'The inhabitants are a tall, majestic people, so unlike the inhabitants of earth. Sin has never entered here.' It was evident from Brother Bates's smiling face that his past doubts in regard to the source of her visions were fast leaving him. We all knew that Captain Bates was a great lover of astronomy, as he would often locate many of the heavenly bodies for our instruction. When Sister White replied to his questions, after the vision, saying that she had never studied or otherwise received knowledge in this direction, he was filled with joy and happiness. He praised God, and expressed his belief that this vision concerning the planets was given that he might never again doubt."—Mrs. Truesdail's letter of Jan. 27, 1891.

I find no reference here to a meal, by the way. We should also note that two pages earlier, Loughborough tells the story of the vision. In his account of it, he never claims that Mrs. White named the planets she saw. Rather, he quotes Joseph Bates as saying so as she described what she saw, "Oh, she is viewing Jupiter!" Then, when she described a planet with belts and rings, and she said,

"I see seven moons," Bates exclaimed, "She is describing Saturn." Mrs. Truesdail's account corresponds to this. She, too, does not say that Mrs. White identified the planets by name. No doubt she accepted Bates's identity of these planets and assumed it to be their true identity.

We have no reason to doubt the legitimacy of Mrs. Truesdail's letter or to question the veracity of its author on these points. But we need to recognize which pieces of information came from Mrs. White and which came from Bates. Others, too, appear to have accepted Bates's identification. In *A Word to the Little Flock,* James White refers to this vision and mentions Jupiter and Saturn. I wouldn't be surprised if Mrs. White herself accepted Bates's judgment on this, since apparently she was not told the planets' identities.

I believe that Mrs. White was shown the things she described and that they correspond to the reality on some planets. But I don't think those planets were Jupiter and Saturn, despite the fact that Bates thought they were. And we mustn't pin Bates's mistaken assumption on Mrs. White.

By the way, there is some brief material about this vision on the Ellen G. White Estate Web site. It's in the "Comments Regarding Unusual Statements Found in Ellen G. White's Writings" section, under "Astronomical Statements."

Question 16:
How could a true prophet have proclaimed the shut-door doctrine?
("Ellen G. White and Shut Door")

> *I find the shut-door doctrine impossible to reconcile with a true prophet. Ellen White said an angel showed her that the door of salvation was closed in 1844.*

I don't think you will find a statement that says exactly what you have expressed here. This is someone's understanding of what Mrs. White said, and such summaries may or may not represent what she actually said or meant.

It seems clear that during the years between 1844 and 1851, the term *shut door* began to shift in meaning. Mrs. White's critics, I believe, fail to take that shift into account, and they quote every reference by Mrs. White to the "shut door" as though these words referred to the close of probation (the shutting of the "door of mercy") for the entire world. Though evidence from those early years is sparse, what there is will support the viewpoint I've expressed.

In the last two months or so before October 22, 1844, the Millerite believers had proclaimed with power the message, "Behold, the bridegroom cometh; go ye out to meet him" (Matthew 25:6, KJV). In the parable, this cry went up at midnight, so the message they proclaimed that Jesus was to return on October 22 became known as "the Midnight Cry." In the same parable, you will recall, those who were ready for the bridegroom's arrival went in with him, "and the door was shut" (verse 10, KJV). So, both the terms *Midnight Cry* and *shut door* came from the same parable.

After the Disappointment on October 22, those who believed that God had been leading in the 1844 movement concluded that they must even yet be just on the verge of the coming of Jesus, and the scorn of the world around them convinced them that they were in the time spoken of in Jesus' parable when "the door was shut." They believed it was too late for sinners to accept Jesus' offer of salvation; in fact, they saw no evidence that the Holy Spirit was striving with the world at all.

In that situation, to give up on the shut door was to renounce one's faith in the Midnight Cry—the Advent movement—and to say that God must not have been leading in the study of the prophecies that had so captivated them.

It was to say that nothing happened in 1844. (Mrs. White admits, understandably, that she came to that unhappy conclusion herself for a brief time after the Disappointment.)

God did not reveal everything to them all at once, even as He did not immediately reveal everything about the resurrection of Jesus to His disappointed disciples, who were mourning and confused over the death of their Lord. (See *The Great Controversy,* pages 404–408.) Though the gift of prophecy was active in the church through Ellen G. White, God allowed incorrect ideas to exist in the church and even in His prophet until He saw fit to correct them.

Ellen White's first vision did not explain everything about the Disappointment, but it did give the disappointed ones God's assurance that they had not been deceived. (See *Life Sketches,* pages 64–68. Of course, she was Ellen Harmon at the time, not yet having married James White.) Jesus was still leading His people along the narrow path high above the world that led to the City of God. There was a light behind them that lit the path all the way to the city. That light, Ellen White saw, was the Midnight Cry, which was the message pointing to October 22, 1844. So the Millerites had not been deluded! On the strength of this assurance and the many other evidences they had of God's having led them, those who still believed could not turn their backs on the shut-door message.

At first they saw their work as focusing on those who had accepted the message of the Millerite movement and who now needed to see the new things God was making known from His Word—matters such as the Sabbath and the sanctuary. They regarded those who had rejected the Millerite message as comprising the "wicked world which God had rejected" (*Selected Messages,* 1:62). But as early as 1845, and much more by the end of the 1840s and the early 1850s, they began to see evidence that people who had not been touched by the Millerite movement were showing interest in their message. This could only be the work of the Holy Spirit, and so it must not be too late for these people. Evidently, then, the door was not yet shut for everyone. The Adventist believers began to see that God was opening a new mission for them. By 1851, this was quite clear to them. Mrs. White had an important role in bringing about this change of view.

As I mentioned earlier, after the Disappointment, Ellen G. White herself gave up on the idea that the door was shut in the past and looked for it in the future—that is, she believed for a brief time that the 2,300 days had not yet ended. But her faith in the 1844 movement revived as a result of her first vision. A superficial reading of what she wrote about that vision might lead one to conclude that the vision taught that it was too late for everyone outside the Millerite movement, but a closer reading will show that this is not necessarily so. She did refer to the impossibility of salvation for "all the wicked world which God had rejected," but while she herself believed for a time that this referred to nearly all non-Millerites, it later became clear to her that the rejected group was quite a bit smaller than this. While there was a door in heaven that was shut by the One who "shutteth, and no man openeth" (Revelation 3:7, KJV), there was also an "open door, [which] no man can shut" (verse 8, KJV). Here was scriptural reference to a shut door that evidently did not mean that probation for all the world had closed.

It should not surprise us that a prophet of God does not know all the truth immediately upon receiving the prophetic call or even after receiving some early instruction from God on a specific point. The prophet may not immediately understand the instruction correctly or fully (see, for example, 1 Peter 1:10–12). The full import of God's message through Ellen White's early visions unfolded over time, and the visions have stood the test of time.

In addition to the paragraphs above, the Ellen G. White Estate Web site also contains a statement Ellen White wrote in 1883 regarding her relationship to the shut-door doctrine and a chapter on the subject from Arthur White's biography of Ellen White. And it recommends what Herbert E. Douglass wrote about the shut door in his book *Messenger of the Lord.*

Question 17:
Was Ellen White wrong about a temple in the New Jerusalem?
("The Temple in the New Jerusalem")

> *I have been approached by a person who read* Early Writings *and is questioning the matter of Ellen White's seeing a temple in the New Jerusalem in her vision. This person is asking how Mrs. White could have seen a temple there when John the revelator says there wasn't one in that city (Revelation 21:22). The vision is described in* Early Writings, *page 32, paragraph 2, and on.*

The answer to your question is actually quite clear biblically. Revelation 21 describes events that happen after the final destruction of sin (depicted in Revelation 20). When there is no more sin, there is no more need of a temple. But while sin remains, there is a temple with its ministry for dealing with sin. This is what Hebrews refers to in places such as Hebrews 8:1, 2 and 9:11ff.

Jesus is now our High Priest in the heavenly sanctuary (or temple), applying the benefits of His atoning sacrifice to our cases and wrapping up the final issues in the great controversy. In *Early Writings,* Mrs. White was shown the present situation—not the one that will exist after the destruction of sin. So her view of the heavenly sanctuary is in line with what the Bible teaches on this subject.

Question 18:
Was a picture of Ellen White wearing a necklace "doctored"?
("A Picture That Shows Mrs. White With a Necklace?")

> *I heard from a pastor that there is a picture that shows Mrs. White with a necklace, but that someone removed—airbrushed—the necklace from the picture.*

I have to smile at how stories grow! There is a 1913 family picture in which Ellen White appears, which was treated this way when it was first published, probably in the 1930s or so. The airbrushing, however, was not done on Mrs. White but on one of her granddaughters—Ella White Robinson.

I have seen the picture both "before" and "after." In the original picture, Ella appears to be wearing a necklace of small shells, similar to the kind of thing our family bought as a souvenir when we were in Hawaii, where such a string of shells or flowers is called a *lei* and is often worn even by Adventist women there.

Ella, a daughter of W. C. White, had lived in Australia during some of the years Mrs. White was there, 1891–1900. Whether the necklace—or lei—came from Australia or from one of the island stops on their voyage home, I don't know. But a published report that Mrs. White bought it for her has no documentation that I am aware of to back it up. So that's the story of the "airbrushed necklace."

See also the following question and answer.

Question 19:
Did a photographer catch Ellen White wearing a gold chain?
("A Picture of Ellen G. White With a Gold Chain and a Brooch On")

> *A non-Adventist relative of mine who was raised as an Adventist has challenged me about Ellen White. She used a Web site as support for abandonment of Ellen White's teachings. On this Web site is a photograph of Ellen White wearing a gold chain and a brooch. What can you tell me about this picture?*

I looked at the Web page you mentioned and found that it referenced the Ellen G. White Estate branch at Andrews as the source of the photo. At the Andrews branch we have this photograph in a display album that we show people who visit us. I looked at that copy and could see clearly that it is not a gold chain Mrs. White is wearing, but a cord with a metal clip at each end. The upper part attaches to her clothing, perhaps to a button, and the lower end I assume attaches to a pocket watch that is out of sight in the shadow of the picture, presumably in a pocket.

However, the picture we display is a reproduction. So I decided to search further to see whether we have an original, and I did find an original print with the photographer's name and address still on it. The picture is very clear—it is a cord, not a gold chain.

I cannot account for why it looks like it could be a chain in the picture on the Web site. In the original picture, though, one can barely see the loop of cord that goes back toward her elbow to where it ends, presumably in a watch pocket. But on the Web site the loop is much lighter, as though it is reflective metal. This makes me think that someone has altered the picture to make it look like she is wearing a chain.

In the photo, Mrs. White is wearing a small pin at the closure of her collar. I think this was not unusual for her, and it seems not to have been the kind of ornamentation that she objected to. Regarding the wearing of a pin, she wrote the following in a letter to her son and daughter-in-law:

> Sister Kerr took me into her parlor bedroom, and opened a box of ruches [strips of lace, net, ribbon, or the like used in place of a collar

or cuff] for the neck, and desired me to accept the entire box. Her husband is a merchant in Honolulu, and though not a believer, he is a very liberal man. She also presented me with three yards and a half of silk, costing three dollars a yard with which I was to make a sack [a short coat or jacket fitting somewhat loosely]. I saw that she was very desirous that I should have this, and I could not refuse without greatly disappointing her. It was beautiful silk left from a dress which she had. She also gave me a silk scarf, and a ten dollar pin, composed of white stones, very plain and serviceable. I thought I could not accept this, but she looked so sorry, that I finally did take it, and have worn it ever since, for it is handy and becoming, while it is not showy at all.—Letter 32a, 1891, pp. 2, 3. (To J. E. and Emma White, December 7, 1891.) [*Manuscript Releases,* 8:449].

As I read the statement, I find three criteria for such things. An item like this should serve a needed function ("serviceable," "handy"), it should be artistically pleasing ("becoming"), and it should be plain and modest ("not showy at all"). Those sound like good Christian principles to me. And despite the Web site's claims for the picture you referred to, Mrs. White's attire in that photograph complies with these standards.

See also the preceding question and answer.

Question 20:
Did Ellen White condemn the doctrine of the Trinity?
("The Pioneers and the Trinity")

> *I'm wondering about the Trinity. I have a friend who has been hand-ing me a lot of booklets that say that thinking of the Holy Spirit as a Third Person is dangerous and that Adventists haven't always held this view. She states that Ellen and James White were not Trinitarians. Can you help me understand what our beliefs are and have been in the past?*

James White would not have considered himself a Trinitarian, nor would others of our early pioneers. In at least some cases (James White included here), they seem to have been objecting to the idea, apparently held by some Trinitarians, that God is really only one Person who has appeared at different stages of earth's existence as Father or Son or Holy Spirit. James White believed that They were separate Beings, so that in Gethsemane and on the cross the Son could actually pray to the Father, not to Himself.

However, various statements from Mrs. White uphold the eternal, self-existent nature of the Son and the full personality of the Holy Spirit. Some of these statements are conveniently collected in the book *Evangelism,* pages 613–617. I've copied some of them and a statement from *The Desire of Ages* at the end of this response.

However, as clear as Mrs. White's statements are, the Bible is the source of Adventist belief in the Trinity. Several lines of evidence in the Bible provide firm support for this doctrine. The Father, of course, is not in doubt here—He is included as God in everyone's list. But the Bible makes Jesus equal with God; see, for example, such texts as John 5:17, 18; 8:58, 59; Philippians 2:6; and the many texts that call Jesus "Lord," which is the term used in the Greek translation of the Old Testament to refer to God. Likewise, the Holy Spirit is called a Person and is equated with God; see, for example, Acts 5:3, 4, where the Holy Spirit is identified as a Person because He can be lied to, and where lying to the Holy Spirit is equated with lying to God.

So, the Bible indicates that the Father, Son, and Holy Spirit are three sepa-rate Persons, yet it also says there is one God (as in Deuteronomy 6:4). How can we account for this? Frankly, it's more than human minds can grasp—but that shouldn't surprise us, for God must surely be greater than our minds can encompass. We express these Bible truths about God by using the term *Trinity,* which signifies a unity of three. I can't find a satisfactory way of accounting for all the Bible evidence other than by this means, which is why I believe in a Trinity.

Some Ellen G. White statements:

> There are three living persons of the heavenly trio; in the name of these three great powers—the Father, the Son, and the Holy Spirit—those who receive Christ by living faith are baptized. . . .—*Special Testimonies,* Series B, No. 7, pp. 62, 63. (1905). . . .

> Christ is the pre-existent, self-existent Son of God. . . . In speaking of his pre-existence, Christ carries the mind back through dateless ages. He assures us that there never was a time when He was not in close fellowship with the eternal God. . . .—*Signs of the Times,* Aug. 29, 1900. . . .

> He was equal with God, infinite and omnipotent. . . . He is the eternal, self-existent Son.—Manuscript 101, 1897. . . .

> While God's Word speaks of the humanity of Christ when upon this earth, it also speaks decidedly regarding His pre-existence. The Word existed as a divine being, even as the eternal Son of God, in union and oneness with His Father. From everlasting He was the Mediator of the covenant, the one in whom all nations of the earth, both Jews and Gentiles, if they accepted Him, were to be blessed. "The Word was with God, and the Word was God." Before men or angels were created, the Word was with God, and was God.—*Review and Herald,* April 5, 1906. . . .

> Jesus declared, "I am the resurrection, and the life." In Christ is life, original, unborrowed, underived. "He that hath the Son hath life." The divinity of Christ is the believer's assurance of eternal life. —*The Desire of Ages,* p. 530 (1898). . . .

> We need to realize that the Holy Spirit, who is as much a person as God is a person, is walking through these grounds.—Manuscript 66, 1899. (From a talk to the students at the Avondale School.) . . .

> The Holy Spirit has a personality, else He could not bear witness

to our spirits and with our spirits that we are the children of God. He must also be a divine person, else He could not search out the secrets which lie hidden in the mind of God. "For what man knoweth the things of a man, save the spirit of man which is in him? even so the things of God knoweth no man, but the Spirit of God." *Manuscript* 20, 1906. [The preceding Ellen G. White statements are all found in the book *Evangelism,* pages 615–617.]

Sin could be resisted and overcome only through the mighty agency of the Third Person of the Godhead, who would come with no modified energy, but in the fullness of divine power. It is the Spirit that makes effectual what has been wrought out by the world's Redeemer (*The Desire of Ages,* 671).

See also the following question and answer.

Question 21:
Did someone sneak Trinity statements into Ellen White's books?
("Question About Writings Being Changed")

> *There is a group of people here who are rejecting the Trinity doctrine and saying that anything in Mrs. White's writings that suggests there are Three Persons to the Godhead was added by Elder Froom after her death. They say that these statements were not in the original transcripts. These folks also say that unless I reject this doctrine, my salvation is in jeopardy. Their reasoning is that I am worshiping other gods and, therefore, breaking the first commandment. I need to know if their claim about Mrs. White's writings being changed to include this belief is true.*

It saddens me to see how people will try to discredit the published writings of Mrs. White when those writings do not agree with their own ideas. Elder Froom had no authority to alter the writings of Mrs. White after her death, and the trustees, including W. C. White, and Arthur L. White after him, did not permit such things to take place.

You are probably aware of a collection of statements with bearing on the Trinity issue that appears in the book *Evangelism,* on pages 613–617. One of those statements, on the divinity and personality of the Holy Spirit, appears on pages 616, 617. Those who deny the Trinity doctrine typically say that the Holy Spirit is not a Person, an individual Member of the Godhead; rather, He is some expression of the power or personality of God. Mrs. White's statement clearly differs from that view.

Did she write it? You can see it in her own handwriting on our Web site. From the homepage, click on "From the Vault" in the lower right corner. Then scroll down to the bottom of the current feature to find the previous features accessible there. Click on the "Blank Diary/Journals" link, and it will take you to a picture of this material in Mrs. White's own handwriting. Click on the picture to enlarge it for easier reading. It didn't come from Elder Froom.

I am sorry that you are faced with this difficulty. May the Lord give you grace to uphold truth and to do so in the proper spirit.

("Question About Writings Being Changed [2]")

> *Is it possible to see other quotes in the original? I'm referring to the other quotes given in* Evangelism: Special Testimonies, *series B, number 7, pages 62, 63: "There are three living Persons of the heavenly trio",* Manuscript 66, 1899: "We need to realize that the Holy Spirit who is as much a person as God is a person is walking through these grounds"; *Special Testimonies, *series A, number 10, page 37 (1897): "Held in check by the power of God in the third person of the Godhead, the Holy Spirit"; *Special Testimonies, *series B, number 7, page 51: "We are to cooperate with the three highest powers in heaven."*

You need to recognize the nature of what you are trying to do. Those who make such a life-and-death issue of the Trinity question must construct a conspiracy theory in order to maintain their belief. In this case, they are convinced that Elder Froom is the main conspirator who has altered Mrs. White's writings so that one cannot believe the printed materials. It is impossible to disprove a conspiracy because those who wish to believe in it simply widen the conspiracy to include those who show them contrary evidence. In their view, it is all tainted. What cannot be wrong is their own idea.

Some of what you have asked for, of course, is published material. *Special Testimonies,* series B, number 7, was published in 1906 and is photoreproduced in the *Series B* volume published by Leaves-of-Autumn Books. I mention this because Elder Froom was born in 1890, and at the time this material was first published he was sixteen years old. It is quite clear that he didn't alter it then, and what appears in *Evangelism* reflects word for word what was published in that tract in 1906. I have verified the quotations you asked about from pages 51, 62, and 63 myself, as anyone can do with the Leaves-of-Autumn reprint volume. I have also verified the quote you asked about from series A, number 10, page 37. You have quoted it exactly as it appears there. As you indicated, this was published in 1897. Elder Froom was seven years old at the time.

See also the preceding question and answer.

Question 22:
Have the most important books Ellen White wrote been changed?
("Books Changed?")

Do you have an official response to the allegations that the major Ellen G. White books have been changed?

The author you referred to who charged the church with making changes in Ellen G. White's writings seems to have a number of things confused. The General Conference action he cites to show that the leadership changed *The Great Controversy* actually dates from a year before his preferred edition of *The Great Controversy* was even written! How could they vote to change it before she wrote it?

Actually, the vote he cited had nothing to do with *The Great Controversy*. It had to do with the *Testimonies*. We have all the original *Testimony* publications here, and the haste with which especially the early ones were published (and which the General Conference action refers to) does show. They needed corrections to bring them up to standard. The General Conference went on record expressing its belief that inspiration extends to the thoughts of the writer rather than to a dictation of the exact words the writer is to use. This is what Mrs. White believed as well. She offered no objection to the revision. The work was done largely by Marian Davis.

You can find what Mrs. White wrote to Uriah Smith about the revision of the *Testimonies* in *Selected Messages,* book 3, pages 96–98. I will quote parts of three paragraphs for you here from page 97:

> As far as possible every defect should be removed from all our publications. As the truth should unfold and become widespread, every care should be exercised to perfect the works published. . . .

> Where the language used is not the best, I want it made correct and grammatical, as I believe it should be in every case where it can be without destroying the sense. . . .

> My mind has been exercised upon the question of the *Testimonies* that have been revised. We have looked them over more critically. I cannot see the matter as my brethren see it. I think the

changes will improve the book. If our enemies handle it, let them do so.

Now, what about *The Great Controversy*? Actually, the 1884 edition was itself a revision. Mrs. White's first *The Great Controversy* was 219 pages long and was published in 1858. It took the story from the fall of Lucifer to the end of time. Today, we call it *Spiritual Gifts,* book 1. Mrs. White expanded the story in books 3 and 4, published in 1864. Then in the 1870s, she set out to expand it some more. She published volumes 1–3 of the set now called *The Spirit of Prophecy* in the 1870s, but the fourth and final volume did not appear until 1884. This is the book the critical author seems to think so highly of. It covers the same time period as our current *The Great Controversy* but in fewer pages and less detail.

When colporteurs [literature evangelists] began to sell this book to the general public, Mrs. White felt it would be advisable to tell the story in a form better designed to be understood by the non-Adventist. Having spent 1885–1887 in Europe, she also expanded considerably the part of the book that touched on European events. The result was the 1888 edition of *The Great Controversy.* In 1911, she revised the book to improve references and remove points of needless controversy. This is essentially the edition we use today.

Did Uriah Smith do this work behind her back in 1888 or in 1911 as the critical author might lead one to conclude? No. In fact, since Smith died in 1903, he had no personal input in the 1911 edition at all. In both cases, Mrs. White's own staff did the work under her supervision. She had the final say on changes that were made.

While the critic says only the 1884 edition represented Mrs. White's position on matters, you might be interested to read what she said about the later revisions. This is published in *Selected Messages,* book 3, page 113. The chapter is entitled "Expanding the Great Controversy Presentation":

> In the preparation of this book, competent workers were employed and much money was invested in order that the volume might come before the world in the best style possible. . . .
> The Lord impressed me to write this book, in order that without delay it might be circulated in every part of the world, because the

warnings it contains are necessary for preparing a people to stand in the day of the Lord.—Manuscript 24, 1891.

If you are concerned about this question, you would do well to read the entire chapter in *Selected Messages,* book 3, and also appendix A, which contains W. C. White's account of the revisions.

Note also what Mrs. White had to say about the 1911 edition of *The Great Controversy:*

A few days ago I received a copy of the new edition of the book *Great Controversy,* recently printed at Mountain View, and also a similar copy printed at Washington. The book pleases me. I have spent many hours looking through its pages, and I see that the publishing houses have done good work.

The book *Great Controversy* I appreciate above silver and gold, and I greatly desire that it shall come before the people. While writing the manuscript of *Great Controversy,* I was often conscious of the presence of the angels of God. And many times the scenes about which I was writing were presented to me anew in visions of the night, so that they were fresh and vivid in my mind (*Selected Messages,* 3:123).

It seems that Mrs. White had quite a different view of the 1911 edition of *The Great Controversy* from what the critical author expressed. Whom shall we believe? Personally, I prefer to take the author's evaluation of the book over the critic's.

Note: in 1950, the White Estate board voted to make dated quotes timeless—for example, to change wording such as "four hundred years ago" to "centuries ago," and so forth. And recently, the board voted to remove the word *intercourse*—which in the past people understood as meaning "interchange" or "communication" but which now has primarily a sexual connotation—from *Steps to Christ* and other books as they are reprinted.

Question 23:

Can we trust the compilations?
("Compilations and Use of Ellen G. White Writings")

Our pastor invited a fellow from our conference to a meeting with the elders one night. During this meeting, this fellow said that he felt if Mrs. White were here, she would agree that about 90 percent of her writings are being misused. He mentioned the compiled books, with a specific reference to the book Messages to Young People. *His implication was that the compilations cannot be trusted—that the content of these books has been taken out of context and that a great deal of the material was written in letters meant only for the people to which they were mailed and no one else. Are his views valid? Are the compiled books taken out of context, and should we stop using them?*

There really are two issues inherent in the comments you have referred to. First, would Mrs. White approve of making compilations from her writings, even the unpublished ones? And second, have the compilations been done well, representing fairly her original intent in the individual statements and her overall position on the subject under consideration?

Mrs. White has answered the first question for us. In her will, one of the three things that she specifically asked the trustees of her estate to do in regard to her writings was to see to "the printing of compilations from my manuscripts." So those who wish to say that publishing compilations is an illegitimate use of her writings are in direct conflict with her own instructions to her trustees. (You can find her will in Herbert E. Douglass's book *Messenger of the Lord,* a digital version of which is available on the White Estate Web site.)

The second question, whether the compilations have been done well, is a matter of opinion. I know that the trustees commit the work of drawing together a new compilation to those whose knowledge and balance in Mrs. White's writings they trust. When a manuscript is complete, besides reading it themselves, they seek other knowledgeable people to read it with a view toward detecting any imbalance, bias, or omissions that would reflect on the value of the work. Only when they are satisfied that it fairly represents Mrs.

White's views and makes a worthy contribution to the life of the church do they send it out for publication.

I have heard various people complain about *Messages to Young People.* I have also heard others say how much that book has meant to them, even as young people. I am of the opinion that a good deal of the book's bad press stems from the fact that it tells people truths that they may not want to hear just then. If someone gives the book to a rebellious young person with the idea in mind that this will straighten him or her out, it probably will not be well received. Likely, neither would a Bible. But to young people who want to deepen their relationship with Jesus and represent Him better, the book is a great blessing. In the words of the old saying, the same sun that melts the wax hardens the clay.

Ellen White included her letters to private individuals in the *Testimonies* because she had received divine instruction that the counsel given for one person would benefit others. So criticism of compilations because they contain information originally written to a specific person flies in the face of Mrs. White's own practice. The original sources of the material used in compilations have always been identified so readers can check the context.

Question 24:
Why hasn't everything Ellen White wrote been published?
("Unpublished Writings")

> *I want to add my thankfulness to the Lord Jesus Christ for blessing us with Mrs. White's writings. I cannot get enough! Is a compilation of her unpublished works available? Why wasn't all of her work published? I am eager to read anything that she wrote.*

The White Estate has begun a lengthy project of publishing Mrs. White's complete letter and manuscript file. Much of it has already seen publication in the works she issued while she lived and in the compilations the White Estate has brought out since her death. But the current project will publish the items sequentially and intact, with annotations to help the reader know who is being written to, who is mentioned, and what the situation may be, as far as we can determine. The first volume, covering materials from 1845 to 1859, may be out as early as 2009. Subsequent volumes are to follow.

You asked why it wasn't all published before. Mrs. White never intended for all of these materials to be published. Some of them deal quite frankly with the failings of others—something she didn't wish to make public. Over the years, many of these have seen publication anyway, but without indentifying the people involved. At this point, though, enough time has gone by that it is unlikely anyone will be hurt by the publication of these things, and their instruction may very well help in some situations.

Another reason the White Estate hasn't published everything before this is that the materials contain substantial duplication: counsel that she wrote to one person she might also have written to another, and publishing is expensive. Even so, we feel that the publication of all that she wrote will be worth doing—printing her counsel intact and accompanied by annotations.

Question 25:
Where did the money from Ellen White's books go?
("How Did Sister White Leave Her Estate?")

> *Did Mrs. White get the revenue from her writing or was it all given to the church? Did she leave her estate to her family or to the church?*

Mrs. White used the royalties from her books to pay the expenses of her staff and to finance the typesetting and printing of her books. In her day, the publishing houses did not cover these expenses. She also used the royalties as a source of funds to give to help the various institutions of the church. The church paid her a salary—at first, comparable to that of an ordained minister, and after her husband's death, comparable to that of a church administrator— so she didn't have to live on her book royalties alone.

Mrs. White did not leave her estate to her family or to the church. She left it to five trustees, whom she named in her will, and she gave them specific instructions regarding what they were to do with her writings and how they were to use the proceeds from her writings. When she died, her will provided for some bequests to family and close workers, including some ongoing income from royalties. However, at her death, her estate had more debts than liquid assets, in part because she had borrowed money to give to needy church projects. So the bequests could not be funded at the time of her death. The trustees of her estate worked out an arrangement with the General Conference to borrow the necessary funds, to be paid back at interest from the royalties on her books, and the indebtedness was completely paid off. The trustees made some modest settlements with people named in the will, and no family member or other individual has since benefited from the royalties on Mrs. White's books.

After the death of W. C. White, her son, the trustees entered into an arrangement with the General Conference under which the General Conference provided an annual budget for the work of the White Estate and any royalties from Mrs. White's books went into the General Conference treasury. This arrangement still holds today. The budget provided by the General Conference is substantially larger than the royalty income it receives.

(You'll find more information regarding Mrs. White's finances on the

Ellen G. White Estate Web site, www.WhiteEstate.org. Look in the "Issues & Answers" section, under "Questions and Answers About Ellen G. White." You can read the text of her will in appendix N of *Messenger of the Lord,* accessible on the White Estate Web site in "Online Books.")

Question 26:
Is the inspiration of Ellen White a test of fellowship?
("Ellen G. White a Test for Membership?")

> *When Walter Martin met with leaders of the Adventist Church, he asked whether belief in Ellen G. White's writings was a test of fellowship. Instead of answering his question, the leaders quoted Ellen White herself. Speaking about those who did not fully understand the gift, she said, "Such should not be deprived of the benefits and privileges of the church" (see* Testimonies for the Church, *1:328). Why then is belief in the role of Ellen White included as one of the fundamental beliefs of the Seventh-day Adventist Church?*
>
> *I have asked more than a hundred Adventist ministers if they would baptize and accept into the fellowship of the church a person who didn't believe in the role the church claims for Mrs. White. To this date, I have yet to have one tell me that he or she would do so.*
>
> *Ellen White says that those who do not understand the gift should not be denied the benefits and privileges of the church. Why then did the General Conference president, in an article titled "The Church—Authority and Responsibility" (*Adventist Review, *May 1995), write, "I cannot say that I don't accept this . . . fundamental belief of the church and still claim to be part of the church"?*

I don't have a definitive answer to your question about the fundamental beliefs. As far as I know, this was the first statement of our fundamental beliefs ever to name Mrs. White and to express explicitly that the gift of prophecy was manifested in her ministry. I believe I heard that there was discussion about the advisability of including this point. I don't know what the arguments were that finally prevailed.

Of course, I can speculate. It may be that there was broad recognition that, in fact, this article of the fundamental beliefs does indeed describe what the vast majority of Adventists believe, and it would be only honest to come out and say it. For many decades—perhaps throughout the history of this church as an organized movement—we have held that people considering church membership should be taught about the role of the gift of prophecy among us. We haven't required that people affirm their belief in Ellen White prior to baptism, but our general understanding has been that we ought not to baptize someone who is opposed to accepting her prophetic ministry. This would be unfair to the new member, who would certainly be like a fish out of water. And it would be unfair to the church, which would have a note of discord established within it.

On the other hand, let me be the first Adventist minister to answer your question about baptism affirmatively—with this qualification. In the passage from which you have quoted, Mrs. White indicates the conditions: first, the potential members do not yet understand the gift (they haven't had enough information to make an intelligent choice), and second, "if their Christian course is otherwise correct, and they have formed a good Christian character." (These words follow right on the ones you quoted.) Such individuals are in the category Mrs. White spelled out in the paragraph just before the one you quoted, "Others had no opposition [to the visions], yet dared not take a decided stand in regard to them." This, I take it, was from lack of information about the visions or experience with them. They simply didn't know, but they were not opposed. I wouldn't hesitate to baptize such a person. The baptismal vow in the *Seventh-day Adventist Church Manual* poses the right question: "Do you accept the biblical teaching of spiritual gifts and believe that the gift of prophecy is one of the identifying marks of the remnant church?" If people accept that, then they may join the church if they wish to do so while they examine for themselves the evidences that Mrs. White's ministry was a genuine manifestation of this gift that they believe in and the presence of which they believe to be an identifying mark of the remnant church of the last days.

Lastly, you asked about the General Conference president's statement that people can't say they don't accept this fundamental belief and still claim to be part of the church. Expressing disbelief would be opposition, wouldn't it? Here we have moved out of the realm of uncertainty, of needing additional time to study and to gain evidence. To say, "I don't accept this" is to reject it, isn't it? It is not the same as the group Mrs. White was speaking of, who "had no opposition [to the visions], yet dared not take a decided stand in regard to them."

Regarding the person who refuses to accept after being a member and having time and opportunity to examine the validity of the gift, I would stand with the General Conference president and say that people cannot reject one of the fundamental beliefs of the church and still claim to be a part of the church. "Can two walk together, unless they be agreed?" (Amos 3:3). Such people would be uncomfortable in the church, and the church would be troubled by their influence. If people believe the members of this church are so deceived as to follow one who claimed to have the prophetic gift but who did not have it, why would they want to join them?

For more on this matter, see chapter 2 of volume 2 of Arthur White's biography of Ellen White, and see also the F. M. Wilcox appendix in the same volume.

Question 27:

Did Ellen White forbid preachers to quote her in their sermons?

("The Words of the Bible and the Bible Alone, Should Be Heard From the Pulpit")

> *"The words of the Bible, and the Bible alone, should be heard from the pulpit"* (Prophets and Kings, *626). Are Adventists really using that quotation to say that preachers can't quote the Spirit of Prophecy in their sermons?*

Though some may, indeed, be using this statement for that purpose, that doesn't mean they're right. Taking the statement as forbidding the use of Mrs. White's writings from the pulpit would also forbid the use of the preacher's own words, wouldn't it? Likewise, it would forbid the use of any other writer's words, since "the words of the Bible, and the Bible alone, should be heard from the pulpit." We could do worse than just reading Scripture from the pulpit, but clearly this is not what Mrs. White meant by that statement. Rather, she was contrasting the presentation of Bible truth with human opinions.

Part 2

Questions About the Standards
of the Adventist Church

Question 28:
What did Ellen White say about the wearing of jewelry?
("Jewelry")

What did Ellen White say about the wearing of jewelry?

Mrs. White made a number of references to jewelry. I think the following is among the most memorable. It is found in *Selected Messages,* book 3, pages 248, 249:

> Time is too short to adorn the body with gold or silver or costly apparel. . . . Jesus, the Commander in the heavenly courts, laid aside His crown of royalty and His royal robe and stepped down from His royal throne, and clothed His divinity with the habiliments of humanity, and for our sakes became poor, that we through His poverty might come into possession of eternal riches, and yet the very ones for whom Christ has done everything that was possible to do to save perishing souls from eternal ruin feel so little disposition to deny themselves anything that they have money to buy.
>
> The Lord is soon to come, and His reward is with Him and His

work before Him to give every man according to his work. I try to set before the people that we are handling the Lord's money to accomplish the most important work that can be done. They can, individually, through denial of self, do much more if all do a little, and the many little rivulets will make quite a current sent flowing heavenward.

True, it is difficult for all to take in the situation. Self, self, self, must be served and glorified, and how hard it is for all to become laborers together with God. Oh, that a spirit of self-sacrifice might come to every church, and thus every soul nigh and afar off might learn the value of money, and use it while they can, and say, "Of Thine own, Lord, we give Thee" (See 1 Chronicles 29:14).—Letter 110, 1896.

We have not time to give anxious thought as to what we shall eat and drink, and wherewithal we shall be clothed. Let us live simply, and work in simplicity. Let us dress in such a modest, becoming way that we will be received wherever we go. Jewelry and expensive dress will not give us influence, but the ornament of a meek and quiet spirit—the result of devotion to the service of Christ—will give us power with God. Kindness and forethought for those about us are qualities precious in the sight of heaven. If you have not given attention to the acquirement of these graces, do so now, for you have no time to lose.—Manuscript 83, 1909.

Question 29:
Did Ellen White say we shouldn't wear wedding rings?
("Wedding Ring")

Members of our church want to know what Ellen G. White had to say about wearing wedding bands/rings. Did she say we shouldn't wear them?

There is only one known statement from Mrs. White that explicitly addresses the wedding ring. It is published in *Testimonies to Ministers and Gospel Workers,* pages 179–181. It was written to American missionaries in Australia, where the wearing of the ring was the well-established custom. Here is her statement, with a paragraph or two of context before it:

In eating, dressing, and in the furnishing of our school building, we want to preserve the simplicity of true godliness. Many will deny themselves and sacrifice much in order to contribute toward making the missionary work a success, and should they see this means expended upon the finest linen and the more expensive furniture or articles for the table, it would have a most unfortunate influence upon these brethren and sisters. Nothing could militate more decidedly against our present and future usefulness in this country. The very first lesson to teach the students is self-denial. Let their eyes, their senses, take in the lesson; let all the appointments of the school convey practical instruction in this line, that the work can be carried forward only by a constant sacrifice. . . .

Our ministers and their wives should be an example in plainness of dress; they should dress neatly, comfortably, wearing good material, but avoiding anything like extravagance and trimmings, even if not expensive; for these things tell to our disadvantage. We should educate the youth to simplicity of dress, plainness with neatness. Let the extra trimmings be left out, even though the cost be but a trifle.

The Wedding Ring
Some have had a burden in regard to the wearing of a marriage

ring, feeling that the wives of our ministers should conform to this custom. All this is unnecessary. Let the ministers' wives have the golden link which binds their souls to Jesus Christ, a pure and holy character, the true love and meekness and godliness that are the fruit borne upon the Christian tree, and their influence will be secure anywhere. The fact that a disregard of the custom occasions remark is no good reason for adopting it. Americans can make their position understood by plainly stating that the custom is not regarded as obligatory in our country. We need not wear the sign, for we are not untrue to our marriage vow, and the wearing of the ring would be no evidence that we were true. I feel deeply over this leavening process which seems to be going on among us, in the conformity to custom and fashion. Not one penny should be spent for a circlet of gold to testify that we are married. In countries where the custom is imperative, we have no burden to condemn those who have their marriage ring; let them wear it if they can do so conscientiously; but let not our missionaries feel that the wearing of the ring will increase their influence one jot or tittle. If they are Christians, it will be manifest in their Christlikeness of character, in their words, in their works, in the home, in association with others; it will be evinced by their patience and long-suffering and kindliness. They will manifest the spirit of the Master, they will possess His beauty of character, His loveliness of disposition, His sympathetic heart.

You will notice that Mrs. White did not forbid the wearing of the ring, but said that "in countries where the custom is imperative," that is, where it is a "criterion of virtue" (to use W. C. White's phrase), she had no objection to people wearing the ring "if they can do so conscientiously." By that latter expression, I think she meant that they should weigh the matter carefully, mindful of the possible negative side of wearing the ring, and then wear it only if they are convinced that this is what they should do. Here in North America the more widespread wearing of the wedding ring seems to have been accompanied by the increased use of other kinds of jewelry by our people—rings of various kinds, earrings, necklaces, bracelets, and even various piercings. This is the practical danger that confronts the church.

Question 30:
Must Adventist women wear somber clothes?
("Red Dress")

I have heard repeatedly that Ellen G. White made the statement that every woman needs a red dress. Is this true?

No, the report is not true, but I think I can show you the basis for it. In a letter on this subject (April 29, 1960), Arthur White wrote, "My aunt has told the story of how Sister White once passed along to her a bolt of red cloth for use in making a dress or as she pleased. She has described the cloth as 'red, real red,' not wine-colored or maroon."

Another lady, Myriam Adams, lived for a time in Mrs. White's home while attending our Australian college. About Mrs. White she wrote, "She was kind and considerate in every way, taking the keenest interest in my welfare and advising even in the matter of suitable clothing. She suggested that my frocks should be in suitable shades. I remember one day when [I was] wearing a dark red blouse, she remarked how very becoming it was as I had an olive complexion, and [she] suggested that I should have a frock of that shade in my wardrobe always."

Grace Jacques, Arthur White's sister and a granddaughter of Mrs. White, remembered her grandmother well, since she was born in 1900 and Mrs. White died in 1915. They lived near each other at Elmshaven during that whole time. Mrs. Jacques had an article published in *The Youth's Instructor* of December 5, 1961, entitled "My 'Special' Grandmother." In it we find a paragraph with these words: "I recall a young nurse who had only a few clothes, and so grandmother gave her three dress lengths of material, one of red, one blue, and one a golden color. She told this young lady, as she did several young women, that she should have at least one red dress."

Mrs. White encouraged using good taste in choosing the colors and style of dress (see *Child Guidance,* pages 419, 420). She gave this counsel about having a red dress to some women, but not to all.

Question 31:
What's wrong with going to the theater?
("What Is Wrong With Modern Theater Going?")

What is wrong with modern theater going? If possible, please give references.

Basically, I see the issue as two-pronged. First, the general character of the material presented there, and second, the influence we will exert on others if we go there.

Regarding the first issue, a couple of references come to mind: Philippians 4:8 and Psalm 101:3. How can Christians get their entertainment from watching portrayals of the sins that took Jesus to the cross?

Regarding the second issue, people sometimes say, "I only choose the good movies." Even if that is so, will their example encourage someone else who may not have the discrimination that they do to go to the theater? Will someone else justify going to anything shown because Brother A goes to the theater?

In addition, we must consider the likelihood that the "careful" theatergoers' standards will change by beholding. Will they soon come to think as acceptable a movie that would have shocked them earlier? See Isaiah 5:20. A famous piece of verse by Alexander Pope tells the story:

> Vice is a monster of so frightful mien,
> As to be hated needs but to be seen;
> Yet seen too oft, familiar with her face,
> We first endure, then pity, then embrace.

Finally, the admission that the "careful" theatergoer pays today to see the "good" movie helps to keep the movie house open next week when a bad movie will be featured.

If by "modern theater" you meant stage plays, I think the criteria still apply. More than a hundred years ago, Mrs. White wrote,

> Satan is using every means to make crime and debasing vice popu-

lar. We cannot walk the streets of our cities without encountering flaring notices of crime presented in some novel, or to be acted at some theater. The mind is educated to familiarity with sin. . . .

Many of the amusements popular in the world today, even with those who claim to be Christians, tend to the same end as did those of the heathen. There are indeed few among them that Satan does not turn to account in destroying souls. Through the drama he has worked for ages to excite passion and glorify vice. The opera, with its fascinating display and bewildering music, the masquerade, the dance, the card table, Satan employs to break down the barriers of principle and open the door to sensual indulgence (*Patriarchs and Prophets*, 459, 460).

Many place themselves on the enchanted ground by frequenting scenes of amusement where fallen spirits congregate. Professing Christian, when you resort to the theater, remember that Satan is there, conducting the play as the master-actor. He is there to excite passion and glorify vice. The very atmosphere is permeated with licentiousness (*Signs of the Times*, May 18, 1882).

Among the most dangerous resorts for pleasure is the theater. Instead of being a school of morality and virtue, as is so often claimed, it is the very hotbed of immorality. Vicious habits and sinful propensities are strengthened and confirmed by these entertainments. Low songs, lewd gestures, expressions, and attitudes, deprave the imagination and debase the morals. Every youth who habitually attends such exhibitions will be corrupted in principle. There is no influence in our land more powerful to poison the imagination, to destroy religious impressions, and to blunt the relish for the tranquil pleasures and sober realities of life than theatrical amusements. The love for these scenes increases with every indulgence, as the desire for intoxicating drinks strengthens with its use. The only safe course is to shun the theater, the circus, and every other questionable place of amusement (*Testimonies for the Church*, 4:652, 653).

Has the theater improved in moral quality since Mrs. White's day? Probably no fair assessment of it would say so. If anything, today's theater (whether movie or stage) presents vices more degrading, and more graphically, than the theater in Mrs. White's day ever did.

See also the following question and answer and question 89: Do our angels leave us at the theater door?

Question 32:
What did Ellen White say about Christian drama?
("About Drama in General or Christian Drama")

I would like to know what Ellen White has to say about Christian drama.

Here is the opening portion of a document that deals with that subject:

Inquiries have been received at the Ellen G. White Estate office about materials from the pen of Mrs. White that may bear on the question of using skits, plays, or other types of dramatic programs in Seventh-day Adventist institutions. The Ellen White counsels discussing this question deal with several situations. In so doing, principles are enumerated that should still serve as guidelines for Adventists today.

Throughout the Spirit of Prophecy writings, God has given through Ellen White principles to help us determine what we should do. He then allows us the freedom to best work out our own actions in harmony with these principles. In so doing, it is important to remember that God always points us to the ideal. His supreme desire always is that we reach our maximum spiritually, and in every other way that affects our eternal salvation. . . .

A survey of [Ellen White's] counsels fails to reveal an across-the-board condemnation of all dramatic productions. In other words, Ellen White does not condemn a program just because it may be dramatized. In this respect, counsels touching dramatic productions are much like those pertaining to sports. . . . Mrs. White did not condemn the "simple exercise of playing ball" (AH 499), but as she enumerated the principles involved, she pointed out the grave perils that usually accompany sports activities. Likewise, Mrs. White did not condemn the simple enacted program put on by the Battle Creek Sabbath school in 1888, but in several places she clearly points out the many and almost sure perils that often accompany "plays" and "theatrical programs."

It would then appear that the questions relating to both sports and dramatic productions in SDA institutions must be settled on the basis of fundamental principles rather than on a simple "yes" or "no." This poses a real challenge, one that calls for a careful analysis of the principles involved, plus a determination to be guided by them. If Adventist young people can be taught to understand and apply Christian principles in their personal lives, they will be far ahead of many adults who, tragically, never have learned that the life of the Christian is guided not by arbitrary Do's or Don'ts, but by principle.

For more on these principles, see the previous question and answer and question 89: Do our angels leave us at the theater door? and *Dramatic Productions in SDA Institutions* by Arthur L. White—available on the Ellen G. White Estate Digital Resource Center Web site.

Question 33:
What about dancing?
("Letter Concerning Dancing")

> *I have been told that a woman asked Sister White point-blank if danc-*
> *ing was all right, and she recorded Mrs. White's answer. I would like to*
> *have a complete copy of this article if you are able to access it through your*
> *system.*

The following excerpts come from an article that Mrs. White wrote, titled "Should Christians Dance?" in answer to a letter that asked counsel on this question. The article was published in the February 28, 1882, issue of the *Review and Herald*. You can access the entire article on the Ellen G. White Estate Web site.

> Before answering this question directly, I ask you to consider briefly the position and work of God's people at the present day. . . . The solemn message of the third angel must be given by those who see and feel its truthfulness. The world [is] going on careless and Godless in the way of error. Ministers are saying from their pulpits, "Be not troubled. Christ will not come for thousands of years. All things continue as they were from the beginning." Others pour contempt upon the law of God, declaring that it is a yoke of bondage. But while professed Christians are asleep, Satan is manifesting intense earnestness and persevering zeal. His hellish work will soon be ended, his power be chained; therefore he has come down in great wrath, to "deceive, if possible, even the very elect." Is this a time for us to unite with the ungodly in levity and worldly pleasure? Will they be more inclined to accept the solemn truths we hold, when they see us in the theater or the ball-room? . . .
>
> The true Christian will not desire to enter any place of amusement or engage in any diversion upon which he cannot ask the blessing of God. He will not be found at the theater, the billiard hall, or the bowling saloon. He will not unite with the gay waltzers ["gay" meaning given to pleasure], or indulge in any other bewitching pleasure

that will banish Christ from the mind. . . .

In many religious families, dancing and card-playing are made a parlor pastime. It is urged that these are quiet home amusements, which may be safely enjoyed under the parental eye. But a love for these exciting pleasures is thus cultivated, and that which was considered harmless at home will not long be regarded dangerous abroad. . . . [These amusements] destroy all relish for serious thought and for religious services. It is true that there is a wide contrast between the better class of select parties and the promiscuous and degraded assemblies of the low dance-house. Yet all are steps in the path of dissipation.

The amusement of dancing, as conducted at the present day, is a school of depravity, a fearful curse to society. If all in our great cities who are yearly ruined by this means could be brought together, what histories of wrecked lives would be revealed. How many who now stand ready to apologize for this practice, would be filled with anguish and amazement at the result. How can professedly Christian parents consent to place their children in the way of temptation, by attending with them such scenes of festivity? How can young men and young women barter their souls for this infatuating pleasure?

Question 34:
Are ball games out of bounds?
("Sports, Playing With a Ball")

> *Please provide us with material on what Mrs. White had to say about sports, especially those in which a ball is used. Did she say somewhere that there should be no ball games?*

In light of her statement about the "simple exercise of playing ball," it strikes me that she may have been decrying the effect that the games had on the young people.

> I do not condemn the simple exercise of playing ball; but this, even in its simplicity, may be overdone.
>
> I shrink always from the almost sure result which follows in the wake of these amusements. It leads to an outlay of means that should be expended in bringing the light of truth to souls that are perishing out of Christ. The amusements and expenditures of means for self-pleasing, which lead on step by step to self-glorifying, and the educating in these games for pleasure produce a love and passion for such things that is not favorable to the perfection of Christian character.
>
> The way that they have been conducted at the college does not bear the impress of heaven. It does not strengthen the intellect. It does not refine and purify the character. There are threads leading out through the habits and customs and worldly practices, and the actors become so engrossed and infatuated that they are pronounced in heaven lovers of pleasure more than lovers of God. In the place of the intellect becoming strengthened to do better work as students, to be better qualified as Christians to perform the Christian duties, the exercise in these games is filling their brains with thoughts that distract the mind from their studies. . . .
>
> Is the eye single to the glory of God in these games? I know that this is not so. There is a losing sight of God's way and His purpose. . . . The Lord God of heaven protests against the burning passion cultivated for supremacy in the games that are so engrossing (*The Adventist Home*, 499, 500).

Here is another statement that doesn't seem to rule out games entirely but says that care and watchfulness are needed.

There is great danger that parents and guardians, both by words and actions, will encourage self esteem and self importance in the youth. They pursue a course of petting [pampering], gratifying every whim, and thus foster the desire for self-gratification so that the youth receive a mold of character that unfits them for the common-place duties of practical life. When these students come to our schools, they do not appreciate their privileges; they do not consider that the purpose of education is to qualify them for usefulness in this life and for the future life in the kingdom of God. They act as if the school were a place where they were to perfect themselves in sports, as if this were an important branch of their education, and they come armed and equipped for this kind of training. This is all wrong, from beginning to end. It is not in any way appropriate for this time; it is not qualifying the youth to go forth as missionaries, to endure hardship and privation, and to use their powers for the glory of God.

Amusement that serves as exercise and recreation is not to be discarded; nevertheless, it must be kept strictly within bounds, else it leads to love of amusement for its own sake, and nourishes the desire for selfish gratification. . . .

The training and discipline you undergo in order to be successful in your games is not fitting you to become faithful soldiers of Jesus Christ, to fight His battles and gain spiritual victories. The money expended for garments to make a pleasing show in these match games is so much money that might have been used to advance the cause of God in new places, bringing the word of truth to souls in darkness of error. Oh, that God would give all the true sense of what it means to be a Christian! It is to be Christlike. He lived not to please Himself (*Manuscript Releases*, 2:218, 219).

I recommend reading the section on recreation in *The Adventist Home*.

Note: Arthur L. White, at the time secretary of the White Estate, wrote the following in a letter to an inquirer:

> I am one of Sister White's grandsons. Before I was born she gave to my father a few acres of land which was part of her original home place. She said that he was not to sell this, but it was to be the children's playground and schoolroom. It was just that. We grew up as children playing games and engaging in the various activities about the home and in the garden, all of which helped to make a full and balanced life. In 1902 she gave a certain piece of property to the Sanitarium Church to be used as the site of a church school. There wasn't too much area which could serve as a playground, but over in the corner of her pasture was a playground in which games were played by the church school children. These games consisted of baseball and other games in a simple form as recreation but as it would be for recreation for church school students. There was never any admonition from her that this was not right. [This letter, dated November 9, 1959, can be found in the question and answer file named "Did Jesus Play Games" on the Ellen G. White Estate Digital Resource Center Web site.]

Question 35:
Is there something wrong with using drums?
("Questions on Drums!")

> *Over the years I have heard nothing but bad things about the use of drums in our church. I hear from some sources that the Vatican is trying to "infiltrate" our church through "celebration music," and people link celebration music to drums. If you have drums, you are a celebration church. The thing that concerns me is that the people who condemn the use of drums and other instruments in church never support what they say from the Bible, only from the books and articles that claim this music is part of a conspiracy. But as I have studied this subject in the Bible and the Bible only, I have found that the people of God used many kinds of instruments, even drums.*
>
> *What did Ellen White mean when she said that in the last days there will be "shouting, with drums, music, and dancing" (Selected Messages, 2:36)? I am aware that she was referring to the Holy Flesh movement that was popular in her day. It seems this is the only time she condemns them, and I believe she was condemning how the drums were used, not the fact that they were used. Can you give me more information on this subject?*

Along with you, I don't have much confidence in the conspiracy theories. I do not believe that we should let our practices be driven by them because I consider them questionable. I also believe you are correct when you suggest that the issue really is not drums but how they are used.

You asked what Ellen G. White meant in the statement that you cited about drums at the Indiana camp meeting in 1900. It is always a bit risky to venture to tell someone what Mrs. White meant. In this case, we have eyewitness accounts regarding what was going on at the camp meeting. They are illuminating.

> There is a great power that goes with the movement [Holy Flesh] that is on foot there. It would almost bring anybody within its scope, if they are at all conscientious, and sit and listen with the least degree of favor; because of the music that is brought to play in the ceremony.

They have an organ, one bass viol, three fiddles, two flutes, three tambourines, three horns, and a big bass drum, and perhaps other instruments which I have not mentioned. . . . When they get on a high key, you cannot hear a word from the congregation in their singing, nor hear anything, unless it be shrieks of those who are half insane. . . .

After an appeal to come forward for prayers, a few of the leading ones would always come forward, to lead others to come; and then they would begin to play on the musical instruments, until you could not hear yourself think; and under the excitement of this strain, they get a large proportion of the congregation forward over and over again.—S. N. Haskell report to E. G. White, September 25, 1900. . . .

I attended the camp meeting in September of 1900, which was held at Muncie, where I witnessed first-hand the fanatical excitement and activities of these people. . . . When these fanatics conducted the services in the large pavilion, they worked themselves up to a high pitch of excitement by the use of musical instruments, such as: trumpets, flutes, stringed instruments, tambourines, an organ, and a big bass drum. They shouted and sang their lively songs with the aid of musical instruments until they became really hysterical. Many times I saw them after these morning meetings, as they came to the dining tent fairly shaking as though they had the palsy.—Burton Wade account to A. L. White, January 12, 1962.

With that background, let me return to your point about how drums are used. When I was in college in the 1960s, I played in the college band. We did a little touring and even played for the Sabbath morning church services in a number of places. Some of the sacred pieces we did included a judicious use of snare drums, as well as bass drum, tympani, and cymbals. I think I recall an arrangement of "Onward, Christian Soldiers," for instance, in which the snare drums helped to provide the ambiance of marching. There was nothing irreverent or inappropriate about this, in my opinion. The music was sacred and dignified. Further, I recall that even Handel's "Hallelujah" from *Messiah* uses tympani. So, in my opinion, the issue is not drums, but how they are used.

The problem in Mrs. White's day in Indiana, as I understand it, was that the instruments were used to stir up an excitement among the people that had little to do with the moving of the Holy Spirit. . . . The type of music used today in some churches may not be just the same as what was used there, but many things appear similar. Dance tunes applied to sacred words, music played loudly, excitement stirred up, and influences from theological currents foreign to Adventist teaching are some that come to mind. In addition, the performances accompanying these songs tend to elicit applause for the performer—like an entertainment—rather than appreciation for God. These things, rather than what instruments are used, seem to me to be the significant issues. If we settled these matters, we would not find much occasion to discuss whether drums are appropriate. I think that would take care of itself.

Question 36:
May we celebrate Christmas?
("Christmas")

> *I have a simple question you might answer for me. I am a Seventh-day Adventist, and all of my life (seventy-six years), my family and Seventh-day Adventist friends have celebrated Christmas. I have many happy memories of this event as a child—memories I will always hold dear.*
>
> *Recently I received an e-mail and the subject was Christmas. In brief, the message wasn't in favor of Christmas. Somewhere in the back of my mind I recall something in the writings of Ellen G. White where she mentioned Christmas and the tree, etc.—not in a negative way, but as a time of turning our thoughts to Jesus and also as a time for families to be together. Can you tell me if Ellen White does mention Christmas?*

I will copy for you some of Mrs. White's statements bearing on Christmas. [These quotations come from the Ellen G. White Estate paper, "A Group of Statements From the Pen of Ellen G. White Regarding Holiday Gifts and the Observance of Christmas." The paper, which contains much more on Christmas, is accessible on the White Estate Web Digital Resource Center site. See also *The Adventist Home,* pp. 477–483.]

> Christmas is coming. May you all have wisdom to make it a precious season. Let the older church members unite, heart and soul, with their children in their innocent amusement and recreation, in devising ways and means to show true respect to Jesus by bringing to Him gifts and offerings. Let everyone remember the claims of God. His cause cannot go forward without your aid. Let the gifts you have usually bestowed upon one another be placed in the Lord's treasury. . . . In every church let your smaller offerings be placed upon your Christmas tree. Let the precious emblem "evergreen" suggest the holy work of God and His beneficence to us; and the loving heart-work will be to save other souls who are in darkness. Let your works be in accordance with your faith (*Review and Herald,* December 9, 1884).

The holiday season is fast approaching with its interchange of gifts, and old and young are intently studying what they can bestow upon their friends as a token of affectionate remembrance. It is pleasant to receive a gift, however small, from those we love. It is an assurance that we are not forgotten, and seems to bind us to them a little closer.

Brethren and sisters, while you are devising gifts for one another, I would remind you of our heavenly Friend, lest you should be unmindful of His claims. Will He not be pleased if we show that we have not forgotten Him? Jesus, the Prince of Life, gave all to bring salvation within our reach. . . . He suffered even unto death, that He might give us eternal life. . . .

Shall not our heavenly Benefactor share in the tokens of our gratitude and love? Come, brethren and sisters, come with your children, even the babes in your arms, and bring your offerings to God according to your ability. . . . Let us, upon the coming Christmas and New Year's festivals, not only make an offering to God of our means, but give ourselves unreservedly to Him, a living sacrifice. . . .

While urging upon all the duty of first bringing their offerings to God, I would not wholly condemn the practice of making Christmas and New Year's gifts to our friends. It is right to bestow upon one another tokens of love and remembrance if we do not in this forget God, our best Friend. We should make our gifts such as will prove a real benefit to the receiver. I would recommend such books as will be an aid in understanding the Word of God, or that will increase our love for its precepts (*Review and Herald,* December 26, 1882).

See also the following question and answer.

Question 37:

How could Ellen White endorse what the Bible condemns?

("Christmas")

> *I am a Seventh-day Adventist, and for more than thirty years, I have cherished Mrs. White's writings. I held them in high esteem as from the Lord. But recently, I have met with a crisis in my faith. According to Jeremiah 10:1–5, we are told to "learn not the way of the heathen" [KJV], by bringing evergreens into our homes and "deck" them with silver and gold. But Mrs. White says that God is pleased when we bring a tree into the church and put on its limbs gifts of money for God. I have never seen Mrs. White in opposition to God's Word before. God was wroth with the Israelites when, after fashioning the golden calf, they proclaimed, "We shall make a feast unto the Lord"! Since when do we as God's children offer Him pagan feasts?*

I believe we need to ask seriously whether Jeremiah was describing the Christmas tree or something like it in the passage you quoted. First, notice that though you have identified the wood brought into the home as an evergreen, the Bible text does not do so. It merely refers to a tree.

Second, what then is done with the tree? Are silver and gold hung on its branches? *The New American Standard Bible* (NASB)—a conservative and quite literal translation—renders verse 3 this way: "The customs of the peoples are delusion; Because it is wood cut from the forest, The work of the hands of a craftsman with a cutting tool." It doesn't take a craftsman to cut down a tree. Even I can do that! So why a "craftsman"?

I believe the reason is that after felling the tree, the craftsman carved it into an idol, which the people then decked with silver and gold. This carving of an idol—not the mere cutting down of the tree—required a craftsman's work. Verse 5 actually makes this quite explicit. Again I'll quote from the NASB:

> Like a scarecrow in a cucumber field are they,
> And they cannot speak;
> They must be carried,
> Because they cannot walk!

Do not fear them,
For they can do no harm,
Nor can they do any good.

This is describing an image, a representation of a god, and comparing it to a scarecrow, something that you shouldn't be afraid of! Isaiah 44:9–17 presents a parallel picture, but with more of the detail.

Despite the superficial similarities, Jeremiah 10 is not describing a Christmas tree nor what people do with a Christmas tree. I have seen people in a Catholic church genuflect before the images and before the altar as an act of respect and worship. But I have never seen anyone offer any such homage to a Christmas tree, and probably you haven't either. So having a Christmas tree in the church is not an issue of false worship. Mrs. White, who you have believed was a prophet of God, also recognized that it was not a matter of false worship. Shouldn't we accept her writings when they harmonize with the real meaning of Scripture, as I believe they do in this instance?

See also the preceding question and answer.

Question 38:
May we celebrate Easter?
("Should Adventists Celebrate Easter?")

> *I e-mailed Easter wishes to someone. He replied that we Adventists shouldn't celebrate Easter. But I hadn't wanted to be pagan about it. I thought the resurrection of Jesus is as important as His birth. I know that Mrs. White states, "Christians are making a great deal of Lent and Easter and church ornamentation. It is the old trick of Satan. The Jewish church struck on that rock; the Romish church was wrecked on the same; and the Protestant is fast reaching the same doom" (GC, 387 [1888 edition]). At my church, there were palm branches and the children sang and someone sang the "Via Dolorosa" song, etc. But there wasn't anything that I thought could have been offensive. Will you help me understand this man's comments?*

The Catholic Church allowed for, and perhaps encouraged, the adoption of some of paganism's spring fertility symbols, and they have become a part of many Easter observances. This is the origin of Easter eggs and Easter bunnies, for instance—both the egg and the rabbit were fertility symbols. The very name *Easter* is probably adapted from the name of the goddess Ishtar. Things like this go a long way toward explaining why some Adventists react strongly against Easter.

Though in some respects I share their concerns, I do not share their solution. Mrs. White was opposed to our adopting all the trappings of the Catholic Church and her daughter churches, and most Adventists will agree with Mrs. White about this. But there is never a time when it is inappropriate to acknowledge and glory in the death and resurrection of our Lord, and, it seems to me, especially not on the Easter weekend.

In my days as a church pastor, I always preached a sermon on these things on the Sabbath before Easter Sunday. If that should be the time when a Christian of another denomination entered my church for the first time, I did not want him to conclude that Seventh-day Adventists ignore the pivotal event of the Christian faith—the death and resurrection of Jesus. At the same time, I do not think it is necessary or helpful to try to make our churches as much like the other churches as possible, with the same decorations, banners, ceremonies, etc., as they use. But we can focus on the real significance of those long-ago events. Just as Ellen White counseled people not to ignore Christmas but to discard the elements of it that do not honor Christ, I believe this should be our aim with Easter.

Question 39:
Are Adventists forbidden to have church socials?

("All Forms of Church Socials and Recreation Are Evil?")

> *I have a concern about a comment that goes as follows: "Professed Christians engage in feastings and in scenes of amusements which degrade the religion of Jesus Christ. It is impossible for those who find pleasure in church socials, festivals, and numerous gatherings for pleasure, to have ardent love and sacred reverence for Jesus."—Ellen G. White,* Confrontation, *page 64.*
>
> *An elder at my church who is on a crusade to make Ellen White look like a grumpy, old fanatic says that she was implying that all forms of church socials and recreation are evil. Yet I know from her other writings that she does not condemn wholesome recreation. Please shed some intense light on this passage.*

Mrs. White was not opposed to all such things. For instance, she wrote, "Our social entertainments should not be governed by the dictates of worldly custom, but by the Spirit of Christ and the teaching of His Word" (*The Ministry of Healing,* 352, 353). That is the difference. She condemned the church socials of the other churches that were incompatible with Christian values and standards. She was not here speaking of church social gatherings in which people *didn't* "engage in feastings and in scenes of amusements which degrade the religion of Jesus Christ."

Testimonies to Ministers and Gospel Workers, pages 82, 83, contains the following note about social gatherings. Notice the contrast:

> Gatherings for social intercourse [interchange, communication] may be made in the highest degree profitable and instructive when those who meet together have the love of God glowing in their hearts, when they meet to exchange thoughts in regard to the word of God, or to consider methods for advancing His work, and doing good to their fellowmen. When nothing is said or done to grieve the Holy Spirit of God, but it is regarded as a welcome guest, then God is honored, and those who meet together will be refreshed and strengthened. . . .

But there has been a class of social gatherings in Battle Creek of an entirely different character, parties of pleasure that have been a disgrace to our institutions and to the church. They encourage pride of dress, pride of appearance, self-gratification, hilarity, and trifling. Satan is entertained as an honored guest, and he takes possession of those who patronize these gatherings. . . .

Many such gatherings have been presented to me. I have seen the gaiety, the display in dress, the personal adornment. All want to be thought brilliant, and give themselves up to hilarity, foolish jesting, cheap, coarse flattery, and uproarious laughter. The eyes sparkle, the cheek is flushed, conscience sleeps. With eating and drinking and merrymaking, they do their best to forget God. The scene of pleasure is their paradise.

Mrs. White indicated that Jesus was not opposed to proper gatherings.

Jesus reproved self-indulgence in all its forms, yet He was social in His nature. He accepted the hospitality of all classes, visiting the homes of the rich and the poor, the learned and the ignorant, and seeking to elevate their thoughts from questions of commonplace life to those things that are spiritual and eternal. He gave no license to dissipation, and no shadow of worldly levity marred His conduct; yet He found pleasure in scenes of innocent happiness and by His presence sanctioned the social gathering (*The Adventist Home,* 503).

Question 40:
May we have crosses in our churches?
("Easter")

> *We had a pretty heated board meeting about having crosses in Seventh-day Adventist churches. Does the Spirit of Prophecy have any counsel for us on this matter?*

To the best of my knowledge, this is a matter upon which Mrs. White did not comment. Arthur White said as much many years ago, and I have never found anything in Mrs. White's writings to prove him wrong. However, here is a statement from *The Great Controversy* that may have a bearing on your question regarding the cross:

> There is a striking similarity between the Church of Rome and the Jewish Church at the time of Christ's first advent. While the Jews secretly trampled upon every principle of the law of God, they were outwardly rigorous in the observance of its precepts, loading it down with exactions and traditions that made obedience painful and burdensome. As the Jews professed to revere the law, so do Romanists claim to reverence the cross. They exalt the symbol of Christ's sufferings, while in their lives they deny Him whom it represents.
>
> Papists place crosses upon their churches, upon their altars, and upon their garments. Everywhere is seen the insignia of the cross. Everywhere it is outwardly honored and exalted. But the teachings of Christ are buried beneath a mass of senseless traditions, false interpretations, and rigorous exactions (568).

You will notice in this statement that Mrs. White saw irony, not condemnation, in the Jews' regard for the law and the Catholics' regard for the cross. Just as she did not condemn the law, so she did not condemn the cross; but she noted how ironic it was that those who revered these things did not live by their real significance.

In regard to decorations for our churches, Mrs. White did not condemn such things if they were not extravagant and added beauty or function. Motivation was also very important to her.

Question 41:
Is it a sin to take a bath on the Sabbath?
("Sabbath Observance!")

I found a statement I would like you to comment on. It says something
to the effect that all preparations for the Sabbath should be done on Fri-
day, the preparation day. These preparations include readying the cloth-
ing, cooking, polishing the shoes, and bathing.

While I understand the need for doing all the other preparation men-
tioned above before the Sabbath, I need clarification on the issue of taking
a bath on Friday. Does it mean I'm committing a sin if I take a bath on
the Sabbath?

The statement you referred to is this one, from *Testimonies for the Church,*
volume 6, pages 355, 356:

On Friday let the preparation for the Sabbath be completed. See
that all the clothing is in readiness and that all the cooking is done.
Let the boots be blacked and the baths be taken. It is possible to do
this. If you make it a rule you can do it. The Sabbath is not to be
given to the repairing of garments, to the cooking of food, to pleasure
seeking, or to any other worldly employment. Before the setting of the
sun let all secular work be laid aside and all secular papers be put out
of sight. Parents, explain your work and its purpose to your children,
and let them share in your preparation to keep the Sabbath according
to the commandment.

When Mrs. White wrote this, many people here in America didn't have
convenient means for bathing. Consequently, they didn't do it very often;
perhaps once a week, some more often, and some less. For many people, taking a bath meant first heating the water on the stove or drawing it from a hot-
water reservoir in their cookstove, transporting it to a large tub (in some cases
one that was brought out into a room for this purpose), taking the bath, and
then disposing of the water and cleaning up the area. There was considerable
work involved in it. Some Adventist people delayed doing this on Friday, fill-

ing their day with regular work and leaving the bath for Friday night—after Sabbath had begun. Thus, they had two problems: first, they had a laborious chore to perform on the Sabbath, and second, they were not truly prepared in body and mind to welcome the Sabbath as sacred time when it came.

In many parts of the Western world today, these conditions do not exist. Water is heated automatically and flows into a bathtub at the turn of a valve. It also drains out of the tub with no ongoing effort by the person. These conditions have made bathing or showering a part of the daily routine of many people. In that respect, I personally feel that a morning shower is similar to washing one's face in the morning or brushing one's teeth. There is no labor involved in it, and it does not represent a lack of preparation for the Sabbath. Not everyone sees this question in the same light that I do. I have friends who are blessed in their practice of bathing before the arrival of the Sabbath and then not doing so on the Sabbath hours. I respect and honor their choice in this matter.

In the parts of the world where taking a bath still requires some laborious effort, I believe that it should be done before the arrival of the Sabbath, along with the other preparations that Mrs. White mentioned in the selection you read.

I have shared with you my own understanding of the matter. This is not an official position of the Ellen G. White Estate. I am not aware of the trustees of the White Estate having taken any official position on this point. You are welcome to consider the viewpoint I have expressed, but you are certainly also free to come to a different conclusion than mine regarding how we should apply Mrs. White's statement to our situation today.

Question 42:

Is it wrong to hold church committee meetings on the Sabbath?
("Sabbath Observance")

Does Mrs. White mention anywhere in her writings whether holding business meetings on the Sabbath is wrong—or committees meeting to discuss plans for upcoming events, church board meetings, community service meetings, Vacation Bible School meetings, etc? In Testimonies for the Church, *volume 6, pages 44, 45, she says that instructions in selling Adventist literature and in Sabbath School work and meetings of the tract and missionary societies should not be conducted at camp meetings as this would distract from the spirit of holiness. Would this same principle be applied to the Sabbath? Or are people who raise these issues like those who accused Jesus of breaking the Sabbath and picked at every little thing He did? After all, planning for the distribution of tracts, how to help the poor and needy, how to educate the children, etc., all pertain to Christ and His church.*

You have raised an interesting question. I did not find a specific answer to it in the search I did in Mrs. White's writings, so we may be left to looking at other situations that may more or less parallel the one we are interested in.

When I searched for the phrase "business meeting(s)" in the same paragraph as "Sabbath," I found the following reference from Arthur L. White's six-volume biography of Mrs. White:

The matter [of whether or not to officially organize and register the church so it could hold property securely] seesawed back and forth through the next six months, with some reference to it in most of the issues of the *Review.* Then came the call for a general conference at Battle Creek opening Friday, September 28, to consider safeguarding the work through some type of organization. Because of the importance of the conference, its business proceedings are reported in great detail in the issues of the *Review and Herald* for October 9, 16, and 23. The business meetings began September 29 immediately after the Sabbath, with Joseph Bates called to serve as chairman. Having in mind the debate that had been running in the *Review,* those attending the conference moved immediately into a lengthy discussion. It was clear that most looked negatively on any steps toward organization. Meetings continued through the evening after the Sabbath and Sunday morning and afternoon, ending finally with the adoption of the following: . . . (*Ellen G. White: The Early Years 1827–1862,* 1:421).

The meeting mentioned above had to do with organizing our movement into a legally recognized body. The church leaders waited until after the Sabbath to take the matter up. I am reminded that at General Conference sessions even today, the business meetings are conducted on non-Sabbath hours, with the Sabbath meetings given to inspirational matters.

Yet the point you make about planning for tract distribution, helping the needy, etc., being part of the spiritual ministry of the church seems to have some validity. I don't feel qualified to say that doing such planning on the Sabbath is wrong, but I find myself asking several questions of myself in contemplating this thing: How would the Lord have me spend the sacred hours of the Sabbath in order to best fulfill His intentions for it? Am I inclined to schedule these sessions on the Sabbath so they won't intrude into my plans for the other six days? If I didn't schedule these meetings on the Sabbath, how would I use the time—would I receive more of the blessing that the Lord intends that the Sabbath should bring me, or would I use the time in ways that would result in less blessing?

Question 43:
Should the Adventist Church reject all government aid?
("Government Funding")

There was a discussion in our church about Ellen White's views of government funding of church buildings. Despite searches, I have found no references on the matter. Can you help?

I don't recall any discussion in Mrs. White's writings concerning government funding of church buildings. She did, however, write about receiving grants of land from governments. The primary statements on this point are included in *Testimonies to Ministers and Gospel Workers,* pages 197–203. (See the notes in the appendix for pages 197 and 200 too.) Here are a few selections from them:

January 30, 1895.

You inquire with respect to the propriety of receiving gifts from Gentiles or the heathen. [Cecil Rhodes, premier of Cape Colony, South Africa, had given the Adventist Church twelve thousand acres on which to establish a mission.] The question is not strange; but I would ask you, Who is it that owns our world? Who are the real owners of houses and lands? Is it not God? He has an abundance in our world which He has placed in the hands of men, by which the hungry might be supplied with food, the naked with clothing, the homeless with homes. The Lord would move upon worldly men, even idolaters, to give of their abundance for the support of the work, if we would approach them wisely, and give them an opportunity of doing those things which it is their privilege to do. What they would give we should be privileged to receive.

We should become acquainted with men in high places and, by exercising the wisdom of the serpent and the harmlessness of the dove, we might obtain advantage from them, for God would move upon their minds to do many things in behalf of His people. If proper persons would set before those who have means and influence the needs of the work of God in a proper light, these men might do much to advance the cause of God in our world. We have put away from us privileges and advantages that we might have had the benefit of, because we chose to stand independent of the world. But we need not sacrifice one principle of truth while taking advantage of every opportunity to advance the cause of God (*Testimonies to Ministers and Gospel Workers,* 197, 198).

Our brethren [in Battle Creek, Michigan] are not looking at everything in the right light. [At the 1893 General Conference Session, it had been voted—in view of the denomination's stand on the separation of church and state—to reject the state's exemption from paying tax on the church's properties and to pay the tax.] The movements they have made to pay taxes on the property of the sanitarium and Tabernacle have manifested a zeal and conscientiousness that in all respects is not wise nor correct. Their ideas of religious liberty are being woven with suggestions that do not come from the Holy Spirit, and the religious liberty cause is sickening, and its sickness can only be healed by the grace and gentleness of Christ. . . .

Let these men read the book of Nehemiah with humble hearts touched by the Holy Spirit, and their false ideas will be modified, and correct principles will be seen, and the present order of things will be changed. Nehemiah prayed to God for help, and God heard his prayer. The Lord moved upon heathen kings to come to his help. When his enemies zealously worked against him, the Lord worked through kings to carry out His purpose, and to answer the many prayers that were ascending to Him for the help which they so much needed (ibid., 200).

The Lord still moves upon the hearts of kings and rulers in behalf of His people, and it becomes those who are so deeply interested in the religious liberty question not to cut off any favors, or withdraw themselves from the help that God has moved men to give, for the advancement of His cause. . . .

The Lord God of Israel has placed His goods in the hands of unbelievers, but they are to be used in favor of doing the works that must be done for a fallen world. The agents through whom these gifts come may open up avenues through which the truth may go. They may have no sympathy with the work, and no faith in Christ, and no practice in His words; but their gifts are not to be refused on that account (ibid., 202, 203).

Part 3

Questions About the End Times

Question 44:
Could Christ have come before 1884?
("Christ Could Have Come")

Do you know of any statements before 1884 that say that Christ could have come by that time if people had done their duty?

Here are a couple of references that qualify.

The long night of gloom is trying; but the morning is deferred in mercy, because if the Master should come, so many would be found unready. God's unwillingness to have His people perish has been the reason for so long delay (*Testimonies for the Church,* 2:194). [1868]

The angels of God in their messages to men represent time as very short. Thus it has always been presented to me. It is true that time has continued longer than we expected in the early days of this message. Our Saviour did not appear as soon as we hoped. But has the word of the Lord failed? Never! It should be remembered that the promises and threatenings of God are alike conditional.

God had committed to His people a work to be accomplished on earth. The third angel's message was to be given, the minds of believers were to be directed to the heavenly sanctuary, where Christ had entered to make atonement for His people. The Sabbath reform was to be carried forward. The breach in the law of God must be made up. The message must be proclaimed with a loud voice, that all the inhabitants of earth might receive the warning. The people of God must purify their souls through obedience to the truth, and be prepared to stand without fault before Him at His coming.

Had Adventists, after the great disappointment in 1844, held fast their faith, and followed on unitedly in the opening providence of God, receiving the message of the third angel and in the power of the Holy Spirit proclaiming it to the world, they would have seen the salvation of God, the Lord would have wrought mightily with their efforts, the work would have been completed, and Christ would have come ere this to receive His people to their reward (*Selected Messages*, 1:67, 68). [1883]

These are only part of a longer document that you can read on the White Estate Web site: http://www.WhiteEstate.org/issues/delay.html.

Question 45:
Will the Democratic Party enact the Sunday laws?
("Democratic Party Responsible for Sunday Laws?")

> *A good friend tells me that at church this past week the pastor stated that Mrs. White said it will be the Democratic Party that will be responsible for enacting the Sunday laws. I have been searching on this site for this information but cannot seem to find it. Apparently, the pastor also says Mrs. White stated that the last American president will be born in a foreign country.*

Both of these claims are false. One of them has been listed among the "apocryphal quotations" of Mrs. White's since the 1960s, when the three-volume *Comprehensive Index to the Writings of Ellen G. White* was published. In the back of volume 3, in appendix C, you will find that list of apocryphal quotations. We took that list and added some more to it for our Web site. Under "Issues & Answers" on our main menu, we have a section called "Statements Mistakenly Attributed to Ellen G. White." Here is the entry from that location for one of your questions: "Political Party or Family Name of Last President of the United States. Reports that Ellen G. White indicated directly or indirectly the family name or political party of the President of the United States at the time of earth's closing scenes are pure fiction."

The other claim, which Mrs. White said that the last president of the United States would be born in a foreign country, is equally fictitious.

Question 46:
Will the United States be brought to its knees?
("Before the End of Time, the United States Will Be Brought to its Knees")

I have heard some people say that Ellen White wrote something about before the end of time, the United States will be brought to its knees. Is this correct or is it hearsay? If it's true, where is it located in her writings?

Mrs. White made no such statement. In volume 1 of the *Testimonies,* she wrote, "This nation will yet be humbled into the dust," but the setting makes it clear that she was referring to the Civil War (259).

As for end times, the closest thing I know to what you are seeking is a reference to the United States' "temporal prosperity" needing restoration. Here it is, from *The Great Controversy,* page 590:

> And then the great deceiver will persuade men that those who serve God are causing these evils. The class that have provoked the displeasure of Heaven will charge all their troubles upon those whose obedience to God's commandments is a perpetual reproof to transgressors. It will be declared that men are offending God by the violation of the Sunday sabbath; that this sin has brought calamities which will not cease until Sunday observance shall be strictly enforced; and that those who present the claims of the fourth commandment, thus destroying reverence for Sunday, are troublers of the people, preventing their restoration to divine favor and temporal prosperity. Thus the accusation urged of old against the servant of God will be repeated and upon grounds equally well established: "And it came to pass, when Ahab saw Elijah, that Ahab said unto him, Art thou he that troubleth Israel? And he answered, I have not troubled Israel; but thou, and thy father's house, in that ye have forsaken the commandments of the Lord, and thou hast followed Baalim." 1 Kings 18:17, 18. As the wrath of the people shall be excited by false charges, they will pursue a course toward God's ambassadors very similar to that which apostate Israel pursued toward Elijah.

Question 47:
Will the Ten Commandment ark be found?
("Ark Will Be Found")

> *We are trying to find where it is that Ellen White says the ark will be found sometime in the last days. We looked up "ark" in the index but there was no reference to that statement. We know we have read her saying that but can't find it.*

This question comes up fairly frequently, so some years ago the White Estate began distributing a paper—"The Ark of the Covenant, Will It Be Found?"—by Elder Odom to those who ask about it. The specific question you have asked is dealt with toward the end of the paper. (See below. You can read the whole paper on the White Estate Web site, and you'll find in it numerous statements from Ellen White on the subject.) After reading it, you may decide, as I have, that the case is not so clear that the ark of the testimony—that *is* the one you were asking about, isn't it?—will be found here on earth.

> In examining the teachings of the Spirit of Prophecy . . . concerning the hidden ark of the covenant and the tables of the law of God, it is essential that we keep in mind the fact that there have existed *two* arks of the covenant—one in the earthly sanctuary, and one in the heavenly sanctuary—and that in *each of them* there has been kept a set of tables of stone on which the Decalogue has been inscribed. Both of these arks and both of these sets of the divine law have been hidden from the gaze of men. Therefore, it is necessary to find out which of the two sets of the tables of the Ten Commandments will be brought forth to the view of the inhabitants of the earth in the future. . . .
>
> The set of tables of the Decalogue which was kept in the earthly sanctuary was in the ark when it was hidden by righteous men in a cave shortly before the destruction of the temple by the Babylonians. . . .
>
> "Among the righteous still in Jerusalem . . . were some who determined to place beyond the reach of ruthless hands the sacred ark containing the tables of stone on which had been traced the precepts of

the Decalogue. This they did. With mourning and sadness they secreted the ark in a cave, where it was to be hidden from the people of Israel and Judah because of their sins, and was to be no more restored to them. That sacred ark is yet hidden. *It has never been disturbed since it was secreted.*"—PK 453 (published in 1917); emphasis supplied

According to the Spirit of Prophecy, the time is coming when the tables of stone on which the Ten Commandments are written will be brought forth to the view of the inhabitants of earth. . . .

"When God's temple in heaven is opened, what a triumphant time that will be for all who have been faithful and true! In the temple will be seen the ark of the testament in which were placed the two tables of stone, on which are written God's law. These tables of stone will be brought forth from their hiding place, and on them will be seen the ten commandments engraved by the finger of God. These tables of stone now lying in the ark of the testament will be a convincing testimony to the truth and binding claims of God's law."—Letter 47, 1902 (7BC 972). . . .

"At the judgment this covenant will be brought forth, plainly written with the finger of God, and the world will be arraigned before the bar of Infinite Justice to receive sentence."—PK 187. (From Ms 82, 1899; see RH November 20, 1913.)

Several things should be noted in these statements quoted above. Nowhere is it said that the tables of the law will be brought forth by men as a result of finding them hidden in a cave. In fact, it is clearly stated that God Himself will bring forth the tables of the law to the view of men [Manuscript 122, 1901 (*Seventh-day Adventist Bible Commentary,* 1:1109)], and in one statement Ellen White specifies that "these tables of stone are in the heavens" [Manuscript 20, 1906 (*Manuscript Releases,* 20:68)]. Moreover, the time when He will do this is said specifically to be "at the judgment."

Odom concludes his paper by saying that elsewhere in her writings Ellen White describes two occasions when the tables of stone will be exhibited, each of which could be interpreted as fulfilling the prediction of the revealing of the hidden tables of stone. However, she doesn't say which of these two sets of tables is involved. The first occasion is just before the Second Advent; see *The Spirit of Prophecy,* 4:456, 457; *The Great Controversy,* 639. "Here, again," Odom points out, "it is clear that God, and not man, is the one who will bring the tables to view. The tables of the law will then be exhibited 'as the rule of Judgment.' This will be done after probation has closed for all men." And the second is at the final coronation of Christ; see *The Spirit of Prophecy,* 4:484; *The Great Controversy,* 668, 669.

Question 48:
Did the events of 9/11 fulfill an Ellen White prophecy?
("W.T.C. Prophecy")

In volume 9 of Testimonies for the Church, Ellen White wrote about buildings burning, and after 9/11 my home church came across pamphlets that say that she had seen in vision what happened in this country on that day. Just recently I came across this vision in the Testimonies, *and I couldn't decide whether or not she was actually talking about the World Trade Center or destruction yet to come.*

I have a friend whom I respect greatly—including his deep knowledge of Mrs. White's writings—who believes that Mrs. White saw in vision the destruction of the World Trade Center. But I must disagree with him. Though there are some striking similarities between the events of September 11 and what Mrs. White wrote on pages 12 and 13 of volume 9 of the *Testimonies,* there are also some clear differences. I don't know whether the World Trade Center was ever billed as "fireproof," as Mrs. White describes the buildings she saw. But whether it was or wasn't, it was not consumed by fire "as if made of pitch." Something consumed by fire as if made of pitch is completely engulfed in flames, but the World Trade Center was destroyed by a fire confined to a few floors. This weakened the steel structure and caused the floors to "pancake" down on one another. If I saw such a scene and tried to describe it, I wouldn't think of the expression "consumed as if made of pitch."

Nor am I aware of anything in those events that indicates that the destruction came because "the firemen were unable to operate the engines." Some point to fire engines that were destroyed, thereby becoming inoperable. But that was a result of the collapse; it was not a factor in the firefighters' being unable to save the buildings.

What is more, Mrs. White didn't even claim that the buildings she saw in that vision were located in New York; she merely said that she was in New York when she had the vision. In my view, these are pieces of data that don't line up with the events of 9/11. It seems to me that people have to rely on creative explanations to make those events conform to these descriptions. Personally, I think Mrs. White saw another event, one that is probably still future.

But I haven't ruled out the idea that she might have seen something that took place in the past in some other location (perhaps during the destructions of World War II, for instance), and we simply haven't made the connection.

For me, the bottom line is that events like those of 9/11 should remind us of the shortness and uncertainty of life. Beyond that, they should remind us of statements like the one we have been discussing, which warn of greater destructions yet to come as we near the return of Jesus. They should tell us that time for this world is short and that we have an urgent work to do, especially in the cities, which we believe are destined for destruction. If the Bible and Mrs. White's writings are correct, as I believe they are, then things will not go on more-or-less smoothly, as they have been doing. What happens on this planet in the final movements leading up to Jesus' return will not be pretty. But we have the assurance that things will then get a whole lot better! We may put our trust in Jesus for tomorrow, and we have the privilege of walking with Him and working for Him today.

Question 49:
Did Ellen White connect the Muslims with end-time events?
("The Muslims in Prophecy")

I was interested to know, in light of current events, if Mrs. White had anything to say on the Muslims and their place in end-time events. I know she said the end would come in the middle of a great crisis, and she did not identify what that crisis would be.

Besides one paragraph of historical reference in the appendix to *The Great Controversy,* I could find only one paragraph in Mrs. White's writings that even mentions what we today call Islam. Here is the paragraph:

> The Saviour has said, "He that believeth on the Son hath everlasting life: and he that believeth not the Son shall not see life; but the wrath of God abideth on him." He says again, "And this is life eternal, that they might know thee, the only true God, and Jesus Christ whom thou hast sent." Mohammedanism has its converts in many lands, and its advocates deny the divinity of Christ. Shall this faith be propagated, and the advocates of truth fail to manifest intense zeal to overthrow the error, and teach men of the pre-existence of the only Saviour of the world? O how we need men who will search and believe the word of God, who will present Jesus to the world in his divine and human nature, declaring with power and in demonstration of the Spirit, that "there is none other name under heaven given among men, whereby we must be saved." O how we need believers who will now present Christ in life and character, who will hold him up before the world as the brightness of the Father's glory, proclaiming that God is love! (*The Home Missionary,* September 1892).

That's all I could find. It seems that Mrs. White did not address the issue in the way you asked about.

Question 50:
Will all the Adventist leaders fall in the last days?
("Will Ross Statement")

> *I have a paper that refers to a statement by Ellen White made about the year 1908. While waiting at the Loma Linda railroad depot in the company of Will Ross, Sister McInterfer, and Elder D. E. Robinson, she referred to a terrible storm of persecution that was coming. [Ross's statement claims she said that after the storm those who had been church leaders "were never seen anymore," and new leaders "who had never sought positions before" would take their place.] Can you tell me anything about this statement?*

I have two items here that may be of some help to you. The first is a statement from Arthur L. White, and the second is one from D. E. Robinson.

Arthur White begins by pointing out that the supposed statement is "based entirely on the memory of one man." Then he notes that while the report claims Will Ross lived near Ellen White in Loma Linda and often went for walks with her, she actually was living in Elmshaven at the time and no longer did much walking. "The point I am endeavoring to make," Elder White wrote, "is that as time goes on matters of this kind tend to blur in the memory. Some things stand out in great boldness and other things rather disappear. Copies of the statement from Mr. Ross which we have indicate that this was written out 36 years after the event which he reports. If this is so, it adds to our problem of lapse of time and unreliability of memory."

Eventually, Arthur White turns to what Ellen White actually has to say about the church in the end time. He says that in volume 2 of *Selected Messages,*

> writing in 1893, Sister White describes several situations which she was called upon to meet where individuals were advocating that the church would go to pieces. You will find these on pages 64–66, but I call attention to one statement in particular. She writes of:
>
> "One, Garmire, who advocated and published a message in regard to the loud cry of the third angel; he accused the church in a similar manner to what you are now doing. He said the leaders in the church

would all fall through self-exaltation, and another class of humble men would come to the front, who would do wonderful things. . . .

"This delusion was opened to me. . . . The word of God came from God to me, 'Believe them not, I have not sent them!' "

Then Sister White, in her last message to the General Conference in session in 1913, expressed many times her confidence in the triumph of the church. She made no reference to a situation like that which has been reported to you in the statement from Brother Ross. Her last message to the General Conference in session carried the title "Courage in the Lord." You will find it recorded in *Selected Messages*, Book 2, pp. 402–408. . . .

I would like to direct your attention, too, to the entire chapter appearing in *Selected Messages*, Book 1, beginning on page 176, entitled "The Peril of Extreme Views."

While D. E. Robinson, one of the supposed witnesses to this conversation, was working at the Ellen G. White Estate, he wrote,

Yesterday I received your letter of inquiry regarding an alleged statement made by Mrs. White by a Mr. Ross, of Boulder, Colorado. Am glad that you sought to verify the statement before accepting it as true in all details. . . .

I can say unqualifiedly not only that I do not remember any such statement ever having been made in my presence, or found in the manuscripts which as one of Mrs. White's secretaries it was my privilege to copy on the typewriter or to edit, or to index. . . .

Not only do I feel certain that she did not make such a prediction, but I know that it is not in harmony with her own attitude toward the work, nor in her confidence in the leaders of the church up until the time of her death.

In light of these statements, I would not give credence to the startling claims of Mr. Ross. This is not to accuse him of anything more than an unreliable memory, something that I myself am all too prone to exhibit.

Question 51:
Who will comprise the 144,000?
("144,000")

> *Recently, a minister from the Reformed [Seventh-day Adventist] Church gave some studies to some of our local brethren, and I attended one on the 144,000 because I feel their position is wrong. I wonder if you know of any definitive quotes that could clear this up. As you know, every wind of doctrine is blowing.*

You are right about every wind of doctrine blowing. And some who take extreme or erroneous positions may, indeed, be very eloquent and may sound very knowledgeable on the points that they are belaboring. But this does not assure that they are correct. You do well to be on guard. See *The Great Controversy,* pages 648, 649, for Ellen White's basic statement on this group. What follows are portions of a document that examines certain statements Mrs. White made about the 144,000. (The document is titled "Counsel Regarding the Question of the 144,000.") Mrs. White did not try to define who would comprise this group, and she cautioned others about trying to do so.

> Christ says that there will be those in the church who will present fables and suppositions, when God has given grand, elevating, ennobling truth, which should ever be kept in the treasure house of the mind. When men pick up this theory and that theory, when they are curious to know something it is not necessary for them to know, God is not leading them. It is not His plan that His people shall present something which they have to suppose, which is not taught in the Word. It is not His will that they shall get into controversy over questions which will not help them spiritually, such as who is to compose the hundred and forty-four thousand. This those who are the elect of God will in a short time know without question (*Selected Messages,* 1:174, 175).

> Silence Is Eloquence
> [The following letter from C. C. Crisler, leading secretary in Mrs.

White's office, addressed to _____, president of the Pacific Union Conference, was called forth by a request from him to Sister White for any light she might have bearing on the teaching that the 144,000 will be made up of Americans only, none from other lands.] . . .

Mrs. White instructs me to inform you she has no light further than that the presentation of uncertainties as certainties, and the urging of mysteries as revealed truths, is perilous and leads to disappointment. She suggests building on Holy Scriptures, the true foundation, rather than on personal conjecture. . . .

[She] expressed pleasure over the fact that I had included in my letter to you the words, "On the matter of the exact meaning of the 144,000 Sister White has repeatedly instructed us that 'silence is eloquence.' "

She also commented favorably upon hearing the words with which I closed "So far as I now know, no one knows the full truth of the matter, nor will we know until we are on the other side of Jordan." —Ellen G. White Estate, December 21, 1964; Revised September 1990.

Question 52:
Will the young children of believing parents be saved?
("Concerning Babies Who Died at a Very Early Age")

Please help me find quotes from Ellen G. White's writings about con-
cerning babies who die at a very early age. I'm wondering where she has
written that the faith of parents covers their children so if a child dies say
at age three or six, the child will be saved.

I don't know of a statement that specifies an age for the child who has died.
As far as I know, this is indeterminate in Mrs. White's writings. But here are
some statements that speak to the basic issue:

> The Life-giver is coming. . . . He bursts the bands of death, breaks
> the fetters of the tomb, the precious captives come forth in health and
> immortal beauty.
>
> As the little infants come forth immortal from their dusty beds,
> they immediately wing their way to their mothers' arms. They meet
> again nevermore to part. But many of the little ones have no mother
> there. We listen in vain for the rapturous song of triumph from the
> mother. The angels receive the motherless infants and conduct them
> to the tree of life.—*The Youth's Instructor,* April, 1858 (*Selected Mes-*
> *sages,* 2:260).

> You inquire in regard to your little one being saved. Christ's words
> are your answer: "Suffer little children to come unto me, and forbid
> them not; for of such is the kingdom of God." Remember the proph-
> ecy, "Thus saith the Lord: A voice was heard in Ramah, lamentation,
> and bitter weeping; Rachel weeping for her children refused to be
> comforted. . . . Thus saith the Lord: Refrain thy voice from weeping
> and thine eyes from tears; for thy work shall be rewarded, saith the
> Lord; and they shall come again from the land of the enemy. And
> there is hope in thine end, saith the Lord, that thy children shall come
> again to thine own border."
>
> This promise is yours. You may be comforted and trust in the

Lord. The Lord has often instructed me that many little ones are to be laid away before the time of trouble. We shall see our children again. We shall meet them and know them in the heavenly courts (*Child Guidance,* 565, 566).

I know that some questioned whether the little children of even believing parents should be saved, because they have had no test of character and all must be tested and their character determined by trial. The question is asked, "How can little children have this test and trial?" I answer that the faith of the believing parents covers the children, as when God sent His judgments upon the first-born of the Egyptians. . . .

Christ blessed the children brought to Him by the faithful mothers. He will do this now if mothers will do their duty to their children and teach their children and educate them in obedience and submission. Then they will bear the test and will be obedient to the will of God, for parents stand in the place of God to their children (*Selected Messages,* 3:313, 314).

The parents' course of action is determining the future welfare of their children. If they allow them to be disobedient and passionate they are allowing Satan to take them in charge and work through them as shall please his satanic majesty, and these children, never educated to obedience and to lovely traits of character, will not be taken to heaven, for the same temper and disposition would be revealed in them.

I said to Brother Matteson, "Whether all the children of unbelieving parents will be saved we cannot tell, because God has not made known His purpose in regard to this matter, and we had better leave it where God has left it and dwell upon subjects made plain in His Word" (*Selected Messages,* 3:315).

Question 53:
Will Jesus' last mediatorial work be to save the children of believers?
("Last Mediatorial Work")

> *I was told about the following quote recently and then came across it with a different reference but couldn't confirm it on your Web site: " 'The last mediatorial work of Christ before He lays off His priestly garments is to present the prayers of parents for their children. I saw a mighty angel sent out and thousands of children will remember their early training and be brought back just before probation closes.' E. G. White,* Advent Review & Sabbath Herald, *1890." Did Mrs. White really make this statement and is the reference correct?*

More than forty years ago, the White Estate included this statement in a list of "Apocryphal Quotations" in appendix C at the back of the third volume of the three-volume *Comprehensive Index to the Ellen G. White Writings.* That list was expanded for our Web site (www.WhiteEstate.org), where you can find it in the "Issues & Answers" section, under the subheading "Statements Mistakenly Attributed to Ellen G. White." Here is what the entry says,

> Last Mediatorial Work of Christ. A statement attributed to Mrs. White and bearing various source references such as *Review and Herald,* 1890, 1898, or 1902, to the effect that Christ's last mediatorial work will be in behalf of youth who have wandered from the fold, has not been traced to any Ellen G. White source. Inquirers are directed to the following statements: "When the storm of persecution really breaks upon us, . . . many who have strayed from the fold will come back to follow the great Shepherd" (*Testimonies for the Church,* vol. 6, p. 401). "The love of God still yearns over the one who has chosen to separate from Him, and He sets in operation influences to bring him back to the Father's house. . . . A golden chain, the mercy and compassion of divine love, is passed around every imperiled soul" (*Christ's Object Lessons,* p. 202). "Heaven is waiting and yearning for the return of the prodigals who have wandered far from the fold. Many of those

who have strayed away may be brought back by the loving service of God's children" (*In Heavenly Places,* p. 10).

These alternate passages, which really do come from Mrs. White's writings, may come as worthy substitutes for the one that does not.

Question 54:
Will God send us new light before Jesus returns?
("Question on New Light Before Jesus Returns")

> *Many years ago, I read many of the unpublished writings of Ellen G. White. One of the things I read was that there is no new light that is to be revealed before Jesus returns—that we now have all the light we need in order for Jesus to return. On the other hand, I have some Seventh-day Adventist friends who feel that new light is being revealed and the way the church interpreted things was not right, but now, through new light, we see things as they could not have been seen before. They believe that we need new light regarding Scripture because we're like the children of Israel, who were in error about Christ's coming because they did not have the right light for the time.*

I do not know of a statement from Mrs. White to the effect that no new light is to be revealed before Jesus returns. It seems to me that she always left open the possibility of our discovering new light. During her lifetime she did not dismiss anyone who came claiming to have new light, but rather she told them how to handle it: take it to the brethren of experience, lay it out before them, and let them determine whether they see any significance in it. If they do, fine—look for further opportunities to make it known. If they do not, let it alone. (See, for example, *Testimonies,* 5:293.) These instructions would have been unnecessary if there were no more light that could be revealed.

Mrs. White wrote,

> It is a fact that we have the truth, and we must hold with tenacity to the positions that cannot be shaken; but we must not look with suspicion upon any new light which God may send, and say, Really, we cannot see that we need any more light than the old truth which we have hitherto received, and in which we are settled. While we hold to this position, the testimony of the True Witness applies to our cases its rebuke, "And knowest not that thou art wretched, and miserable, and poor, and blind, and naked." Those who feel rich and increased with goods and in need of nothing, are in a condition of

blindness as to their true condition before God, and they know it not.—*Review and Herald,* August 7, 1894 (*Counsels to Writers and Editors,* 33).

While Mrs. White said we must always be open to new light, she also warned,

Satan hopes to involve the remnant people of God in the general ruin that is coming upon the earth. As the coming of Christ draws nigh, he will be more determined and decisive in his efforts to overthrow them. Men and women will arise professing to have some new light or some new revelation whose tendency is to unsettle faith in the old landmarks. Their doctrines will not bear the test of God's word, yet souls will be deceived (*Testimonies for the Church,* 5:295).

Question 55:
What must we do to get new light?
("New Light, Old Light")

Does anything in Mrs. White's writings say something to the effect that we have to live up to the light we already have or we will not receive new light?

Here are several statements that perhaps offer the kind of content you are looking for.

Let Christians who love duty lift every ounce they can and then look to God for further strength. He will work through the efforts of thoroughgoing men and women and will do what they cannot do. New light and power will be given them as they use what they have. New fervor and zeal will stir the church as they see something accomplished (*Testimonies for the Church,* 5:369).

Here is your danger, in failing to press forward "toward the mark for the prize of the high calling of God in Christ Jesus." Has the Lord given you light? Then you are responsible for that light; not merely while its rays are shining upon you, but for all which it has revealed to you in the past. You are to surrender your will to God daily; you are to walk in the light, and to expect more; for the light from the dear Saviour is to shine forth in clearer, more distinct rays amid the moral darkness, increasing in brightness more and more unto the perfect day (ibid., 5:486).

With some the knowledge of their true state seems to be hidden from them. They see the truth, but perceive not its importance or its claims. They hear the truth, but do not fully understand it, because they do not conform their lives to it, and therefore are not sanctified through obeying it. And yet they rest as unconcerned and well satisfied as though the cloud by day and the pillar of fire by night, as token of God's favor, went before them. They profess to know God, but in works deny Him. They reckon themselves His chosen, peculiar people, yet His presence and power to save to the uttermost are seldom manifested among them. How great is the darkness of such! yet they know it not. The light shines, but they do not comprehend it. No stronger delusion can deceive the human mind than that which makes them believe that they are right, and that God accepts their works, when they are sinning against Him. They mistake the form of godliness for the spirit and power thereof. They suppose that they are rich, and have need of nothing, when they are poor, wretched, blind, and naked, and need all things (ibid., 1:406, 407).

Whenever men are not seeking, in word and deed, to be in harmony with God, then, however learned they may be, they are liable to err in their understanding of Scripture, and it is not safe to trust to their explanations. When we are truly seeking to do God's will, the Holy Spirit takes the precepts of His word and makes them the principles of the life, writing them on the tablets of the soul. And it is only those who are following the light already given that can hope to receive the further illumination of the Spirit. This is plainly stated in the words of Christ: "If any man will do His will, he shall know of the doctrine" (ibid., 5:705).

Part 4

Questions About Health and Diet

Question 56:
Did Ellen White say children shouldn't touch dogs and cats?
("Ellen G. White's Attitude Toward Animals")

A woman in our church says that children shouldn't play with animals like cats and dogs because they are unclean. According to my understanding, Leviticus 11 speaks about eating but not about touching unclean animals. Do you know what attitude Ellen G. White had toward pets? Did she write that children aren't allowed to touch dogs and cats?

I agree with you that Leviticus 11 is directed toward what one eats. This chapter says that people who touch the dead body of an unclean animal are made unclean for a time. I know of no such warning about the animals while they are alive. The camel, for instance, is named in verse 4 as unclean, but God's people were not forbidden to own camels, ride them, etc., which must surely have included touching them. The same principle applies to horses and donkeys. You can't care for such animals or use them productively without touching them.

I know of no statement from Mrs. White that forbids children from having pets such as you describe. Mrs. White herself owned a dog while she was in

Australia. It was a watchdog whom she named Tiglath-Pilesar, probably because he could be fierce toward those he might consider possible enemies. But Mrs. White seems to have felt affection for him, even to giving him that biblical name. I think it must have brought a smile to people! Another indication that the dog may have been special to her is that her friends in Australia devoted a whole page to him in a picture book they gave her when she left for America. Here is what Arthur White wrote about the matter in *Ellen G. White: The Early Elmshaven Years, 1900–1905,* 5:19:

> The brown-toned photographs help to tell the story of the work in Australia. There is the electro-hydropathic institute in Adelaide. There are pictures of neat little churches Ellen White had visited and in which she had made investments to help the companies of believers who needed meetinghouses. There are portraits of friends, and scenes from her Sunnyside home. One page was reserved for pictures of their watchdog, Tiglath-Pileser, at Sunnyside. It will be remembered that parts of Australia had been settled by convicts, and as some of their descendants seemed to inherit the proclivities of their forebears, a good watchdog served a very useful purpose at Sunnyside.

So I find no basis in the Bible or in Mrs. White's writings for forbidding anyone to touch a cat or a dog because it is an unclean animal.

Question 57:
Has the time come for us to stop using dairy products?
("Ellen White and Her Writing on Cheese")

> *There are some who have gone vegan in our church and very strongly discourage the use of dairy products, believing the day is here to make these changes. Are they correct?* Counsels on Diet and Foods, *page 206, says, "I wish to say that when the time comes that it is no longer safe to use milk, cream, butter, and eggs, God will reveal this. No extremes in health reform are to be advocated. The question of using milk and butter and eggs will work out its own problem. At present we have no burden on this line. Let your moderation be known unto all men."*

It is interesting to me that Mrs. White makes this a safety issue. Some Adventists have made it a health issue, which I do not see Mrs. White as having done. By this I mean that she did not claim that dairy products were inherently unhealthful, as some are doing today, but that one day they would become unsafe. You have cited one such statement from *Counsels on Diet and Foods.* Another is found on the same page, just above the one you quoted, in which Mrs. White equates abstaining from these things as bringing on oneself a time of trouble beforehand, and thus afflicting oneself with death. It is in this very context that she warns against advocating "extremes in health reform," as you have quoted above.

See also the following question and answer.

Question 58:
What's the story of Dr. Kress and pernicious anemia?
("Dr. Kress")

I understand Dr. Daniel Kress had pernicious anemia. Do you have any information about the type of symptoms he experienced, how he was diagnosed, and if his anemia was cured by the use of dairy products or the raw egg and grape juice concoction?

My wife, a dietitian, has had a special interest in Dr. Kress for many years. I asked her to respond to your inquiry. Here is what she wrote,[1]

Dr. Kress's experience is a classic example of the premature restriction of diet. He was a Baptist minister who became an Adventist in 1887. He was acquainted with Ellen White and her writings and became engaged in the health message, choosing to interpret her messages to mean that he should follow a vegan diet. In 1894, both he and his wife graduated from the University of Michigan with medical degrees. They served in Battle Creek, Michigan, in England, and then in Australia, always teaching the total vegetarian diet.

While in Australia in the early 1900s, Dr. Kress developed pernicious anemia. Despite anointing, he deteriorated steadily, reaching the point where he made plans for his funeral service and was expected to die at any moment. Then a letter arrived from Ellen White telling him that the Lord had revealed his case to her and had told her that Dr. Kress should get eggs from healthy fowl, drop them raw into the best unfermented wine, and drink that mixture.

The prescription was almost more than he could cope with, for he thought he had been following Ellen White's counsels in his choice *not* to use animal products. But his belief in Mrs. White as the Lord's messenger prevailed—he ate eggs and recovered. He later came back to the States, where he kept office hours at the Florida Sanitarium into his nineties, living to age 94.

Dr. Kress's story is quite a dramatic one—the timing of the letter

1. Edited for publication in this book.

that had to come by ship from the United States, for one thing. Those caring for Dr. Kress said that he could hardly swallow, but that the raw egg in grape juice was something they were able to get down him. His case was the talk of the area, and many visitors came to see the "man who should be in his grave, but wasn't."

Pernicious anemia is caused by a lack of vitamin B_{12} in the blood-stream. It typically occurs in people over fifty whose stomach acid production is very low. Stomach acid is needed for proper formation of the "intrinsic factor," a carrier molecule that hitches onto vitamin B_{12} from food. The combination of the vitamin and the carrier factor moves down into the lower small intestine, where the B_{12} can be absorbed. (Bacteria in our gut make B_{12}, but we cannot absorb it, for it has not passed through the stomach and hitched up with the carrier.)

In the grape juice and egg combination that the Lord told Ellen G. White to pass along to Dr. Kress, the egg would be the source of B_{12}, for that vitamin comes only from animal sources. (Certain forms of B_{12} develop on fermented soy products, but those forms are not func-tional in the human body.)

See also the question and answer that precedes this one.

Question 59:
Is it OK for us to eat cheese?
("Ellen White and Her Writing on Cheese")

> *I have been studying* Counsels on Diet and Foods. *Ellen White says,
> "The effect of cheese is deleterious" (page 236). "[Cheese] is wholly unfit
> for food" and "Cheese should never be introduced into the stomach" (page
> 368).*
>
> *I have been an Adventist all my life, have always eaten cheese, and
> have never seen these quotes before. I have gone to Adventist schools all my
> life also; cheese was served there. I did ask a pastor's wife about this, and
> she said cheese is processed differently today, and therefore, it is acceptable
> as food. Is cheese acceptable for us to eat?*

This is a matter for people to decide for themselves individually. Many
years ago, Arthur L. White wrote the following in a reply to someone who had
asked some questions on this point:

> In the note appearing in *Counsels on Diet and Foods,* it was the
> opinion of the compilers that "ripened cheese" embodies cheeses other
> than the simple articles such as cottage cheese, Philadelphia cream
> cheese, et cetera. Sister White was speaking of the ordinary cheese at
> the time. . . .
>
> You have asked concerning the pasteurized cheeses. Pasteurization
> was not practiced in the time Ellen White was writing. Undoubtedly
> pasteurization greatly reduces the objectionable features of the cheese.
> I know of many careful Seventh-day Adventists who feel free to use
> the pasteurized cheese moderately; in fact, cheese helps to furnish a
> part of the protein which can well benefit the diet of one who uses no
> flesh food. However, at the time Ellen White wrote dairy herds were
> not tested; milk was not pasteurized; refrigeration was practically un-
> known; and transportation was slow. This gave the finest opportunity
> for bacteria to develop in the cheese.

The problems of that time seem to have made many cheeses an acute—as distinguished from long term—threat to health. That is, if the cheese was infected with unhealthful bacteria, one would become sick quite soon after eating it. Today, one does not hear of this kind of problem very much with cheese. Those arguing against cheese today often base their prohibitions on long-term threats such as cholesterol, or concerns—such as allergies—that affect only a relatively small part of the population. Though such reasons have validity, they do not seem to me to be the same thing Mrs. White was concerned about.

Question 60:
Did Ellen White say chocolate is OK?
("Cocoa and UFOs")

On a program, I saw one of Ellen White's descendants—I believe her granddaughter—talking about what was served at Elmshaven, Ellen White's home. One of the items the granddaughter mentioned was cocoa. Additionally, the Adventist Review *included an article about cocoa and referenced Ellen White.*

My understanding is that the Spirit of Prophecy counsels against the intake of stimulating foods. My understanding also is that cocoa contains caffeine and that Ellen White counseled against using caffeine. Please advise me regarding where the Spirit of Prophecy stands on the use of cocoa, a food that contains caffeine.

Also, I was watching the Larry King Live *show. The subject being discussed was UFOs. Please advise me regarding what the Spirit of Prophecy says about fearful sights in the skies as we near the end of time and whether these fearful sights could be UFOs.*

Mrs. White made no mention of chocolate or cocoa in her writings, so I have nothing to offer you regarding her stand on cocoa. As for the caffeine issue, cocoa does not give people a caffeine "kick" the way coffee and other caffeinated beverages do. So it does not seem to be a stimulating beverage. If there is caffeine in it, it appears to be in amounts too small to have a measurable effect on the body (pulse rate, wakefulness, edginess, etc.). In light of these things, it may be best to leave the matter of the use of cocoa to individuals to decide for themselves.

Regarding UFOs, I know of no statement from Mrs. White that might be taken as applying to them.

Question 61:
May we eat fermented foods and mushrooms?
("Ellen G. White's Counsels on Fermented Foods and Mushrooms")

> *I would like to find out what Ellen White has counseled on fermented foods and mushrooms. I am particularly concerned with soy sauce, miso, and tempeh, and even soy yogurt. They seem to be healthy foods, but someone told me that Mrs. White says we shouldn't be eating these.*
>
> *Also, do mushrooms fall into this category? I became very ill after eating some the other day. It may not have been the mushrooms, but my instinct or something makes me think it was. I don't remember ever getting sick on mushrooms before. Again, someone said Mrs. White counsels against mushrooms or fungus foods. I don't want to get weird about the diet issue, but I would like to know if there are counsels on these matters.*

I could find no references in Mrs. White's writings to the "fermented foods" you asked about. Nor are there any occurrences of the words *mushroom* or *mushrooms* in her published writings, and the six references to *fungus* are all metaphorical. In other words, I simply don't find her condemning the foods you have asked about. She didn't address them.

Question 62:
Must fruit and vegetables never be eaten at the same meal?
("Fruit/Vegetables")

Friends and I were having a discussion about eating fruits and vegetables at the same meal. What determines what is a fruit and what is a vegetable? Also, what did Mrs. White suggest on this subject, and where can we find it?

Here are Mrs. White's few statements on this subject, as found in the compilation *Counsels on Diet and Foods:*

There should not be a great variety at any one meal, for this encourages overeating, and causes indigestion.

It is not well to eat fruit and vegetables at the same meal. If the digestion is feeble, the use of both will often cause distress, and inability to put forth mental effort. It is better to have the fruit at one meal, and the vegetables at another (112).

Here is one reason why some have not been successful in their efforts to simplify their food. . . . Food is prepared without painstaking, and there is a continual sameness. There should not be many kinds at any one meal, but all meals should not be composed of the same kinds of food without variation. Food should be prepared with simplicity, yet with a nicety which will invite the appetite. . . . Eat largely of fruits and vegetables (200).

In the night seasons, it seemed that Elder —— was taken sick, and an experienced physician said to you, "I took notice of your diet. You eat too great a variety at one meal. Fruit and vegetables taken at one meal produce acidity of the stomach; then impurity of the blood results, and the mind is not clear because the digestion is imperfect" (112, 113).

Some honestly think that a proper dietary consists chiefly of porridge. To eat largely of porridge would not ensure health to the digestive organs; for it is too much like liquid. Encourage the eating of fruit and vegetables and bread. . . . If we would preserve the best health, we should avoid eating vegetables and fruit at the same meal. If the stomach is feeble, there will be distress, the brain will be confused, and unable to put forth mental effort. Have fruit at one meal and vegetables at the next (394, 395).

Botanically speaking, a fruit is the seed-bearing portion of a plant, while a vegetable may be another portion of the plant.

While all of us may be free to decide for ourselves how to apply these statements, I will simply note that Mrs. White's cautions against eating fruits and vegetables at the same meal seem to cluster around two concerns: too great a variety of food at one meal (which tempts us to overeat), and the needs of some who have feeble digestive organs. Mrs. White herself did not rigidly separate fruits and vegetables in her own eating, for we have favorable reports from her of meals in which items from both categories are named.

In light of these things, it seems to me that those who have either of the two problems that Mrs. White mentioned in this regard would be well advised to follow this counsel. It seems to have been given especially for them. Others may not need to be careful about it, but may, at times, have both at the same meal, as Mrs. White herself did.

Question 63:
Do I have to stop eating meat to be saved?
("Flesh Eating Will Jeopardize Salvation")

We are trying to find an Ellen G. White quote that says "flesh eating will jeopardize salvation." We have tried all other searches and have failed.

You may be thinking of this statement, from *Counsels on Health,* page 575:

> Greater reforms should be seen among the people who claim to be looking for the soon appearing of Christ. Health reform is to do among our people a work which it has not yet done. There are those who ought to be awake to the danger of meat eating, who are still eating the flesh of animals, thus endangering the physical, mental, and spiritual health. Many who are now only half converted on the question of meat eating will go from God's people, to walk no more with them.

Though Mrs. White gave such warnings about the effects of meat eating, she recognized that a vegetarian diet would not be the most healthful—or even possible—in every part of the world. In some places there is simply not the variety of wholesome foods available to sustain the vegetarian. She urged that one do the best one can in the prevailing circumstances. One of the best summaries of her position is found in *Testimonies for the Church,* volume 9, pages 153–166. It was a message she delivered to the General Conference of 1909, the last one she attended. Here are a couple of key paragraphs on the points we are discussing.

> If we could be benefited by indulging the desire for flesh foods, I would not make this appeal to you; but I know we cannot. Flesh foods are injurious to the physical well-being, and we should learn to do without them. Those who are in a position where it is possible to secure a vegetarian diet, but who choose to follow their own preferences in this matter, eating and drinking as they please, will gradually grow careless of the instruction the Lord has given regarding other phases of

the present truth and will lose their perception of what is truth; they will surely reap as they have sown (156, 157).

We do not mark out any precise line to be followed in diet; but we do say that in countries where there are fruits, grains, and nuts in abundance, flesh food is not the right food for God's people. I have been instructed that flesh food has a tendency to animalize the nature, to rob men and women of that love and sympathy which they should feel for everyone, and to give the lower passions control over the higher powers of the being. If meat eating was ever healthful, it is not safe now. Cancers, tumors, and pulmonary diseases are largely caused by meat eating. We are not to make the use of flesh food a test of fellowship, but we should consider the influence that professed believers who use flesh foods have over others. As God's messengers, shall we not say to the people: "Whether therefore ye eat, or drink, or whatsoever ye do, do all to the glory of God"? 1 Corinthians 10:31. . . . The health of the body is to be regarded as essential for growth in grace and the acquirement of an even temper. If the stomach is not properly cared for, the formation of an upright, moral character will be hindered. The brain and nerves are in sympathy with the stomach. Erroneous eating and drinking result in erroneous thinking and acting (159, 160).

In short, we might say that Mrs. White recognized and warned about the physical, moral, and spiritual dangers involved in a meat diet without insisting that everyone in every part of the world must stop eating meat. If meat eating jeopardizes one's salvation, it is because of the natural effects of the meat on the body and the sensibilities, even the moral ones, rather than its being a matter of disloyalty or disobedience to God in and of itself, such as Sabbath breaking or the failure to return the tithe might be.

See also the following question and answer.

Question 64:
Will only vegetarians be translated?
("Meat Eaters and Translation")

I remember reading something years ago in the Spirit of Prophecy, possibly in Counsels on Diet and Foods, *to the effect that meat eaters will not be translated. I am wondering if Mrs. White ever wrote such a statement.*

There is no statement from Mrs. White that says meat eaters cannot be translated. Some people deduce it (wrongly, I believe) from the following statement, found in *Counsels on Diet and Foods,* pages 380, 381:

> Among those who are waiting for the coming of the Lord, meat eating will eventually be done away; flesh will cease to form a part of their diet. We should ever keep this end in view, and endeavor to work steadily toward it. I cannot think that in the practice of flesh eating we are in harmony with the light which God has been pleased to give us.

Some people have turned Mrs. White's *description* in the first sentence into a *prescription*—a *will be* into a *have to.* But notice the lack of any reference to translation. The underlying theme of the paragraph is how to be in harmony with the light God has given us and how to give the right example to others, which will please God. It is not about things you have to do if you want to be translated. The statement contains no assertion that those who are eating meat will have to die before Jesus comes. Rather, I believe, Mrs. White is saying that those preparing for the Lord's coming will want to know what their Father's will is, and it will be their aim to fashion their lives after His design. This emphasis is a little clearer in another place where some of the same material appears, but with an additional sentence of context before it:

> Again and again I have been shown that God is trying to lead us back, step by step, to His original design—that man should subsist

upon the natural products of the earth. Among those who are waiting for the coming of the Lord, meat eating will eventually be done away (*Counsels on Health,* 450).

See also the preceding question and answer.

Question 65:
Must we be "teetotalers" to be true vegetarians?
("Eating What Is Available")

I have been looking for a quote that I have not been able to find. It is about eating what is available, and what is best, but if the best is not available, then it is prideful not to eat something that is less than the best.

Neither I nor a knowledgeable colleague at the main office of the White Estate could think of a statement from Mrs. White along the lines you have asked about. My colleague, however, referred me to Herbert E. Douglass's excellent book, *Messenger of the Lord,* in which Elder Douglass does a good review of Mrs. White's teachings on health. On page 316, we find the following paragraphs:

> In 1894, Ellen White wrote to a non-Adventist active in the temperance cause in Australia who had asked about the Adventist position on being "total abstainers": "I am happy to assure you that as a denomination we are in the fullest sense total abstainers from the use of spirituous liquors, wine, beer, [fermented] cider, and also tobacco and all other narcotics. . . . All are vegetarians, many abstaining from the use of flesh food, while others use it in only the most moderate degree." Many of Ellen White's strongest statements against meat were written after she had renewed her commitment to total abstinence in 1894.
>
> Here we note that for Ellen White a vegetarian was not necessarily a "teetotaler," that is, a total abstainer, but one who did not eat flesh foods as a habit. Here we have a clear example of the difference between a principle and a policy. Vegetarianism was a policy based upon principle: we should eat the best food obtainable under the circumstances. Principles are clear statements, always true under all circumstances. Policies may change, due to time, place, and circumstances. Policies work out the principles by always doing the best possible under the circumstances. Only the individual's conscience knows when

those decisions of doing "one's best" have been made (brackets in the original).

If you do not have Douglass's book, you can access it on the White Estate Web site. On this topic, see chapter 27 especially.

Question 66:
Did Mrs. White's understanding of the cause of diseases change?
("Ellen G. White's Progressive Move From Miasma Theory to Germ Theory")

Ellen White fully endorsed the miasma theory of the cause of disease until the 1890s, when the germ theory became more commonly accepted. The difference is evident in the establishment of Adventist medical schools. For the Battle Creek medical school, she promoted the idea of prospective instructors being trained in the use of "natural remedies" and water treatments—basics of the naturopathic schools of the day.

When the medical school was established in Loma Linda in the early twentieth century, naturopathic colleges were increasing until in 1930 there were twenty, with more than ten thousand practicing naturopaths in the United States. But Ellen White had by then adopted the emerging germ theory and directed that the college at Loma Linda should become fully licensed as an allopathic medical school. Her prophecy that this college and its graduates would become the envy of other denominations has certainly been fulfilled. That would not be so today if we did not accept the principle that our understandings on the subjects of health are continually progressive.

While there are many problems with modern medical procedures, there is much more gain than loss. And to revert to nineteenth-century medicine based on Ellen White's understanding at the time is unfortunate and detrimental to the progress of our spiritual message. "The truth of God is progressive; it is always onward, going from strength to a greater strength, from light to a greater light" [Signs of the Times, May 26, 1890]. "Let the diet reform be progressive" [Testimonies for the Church, 7:135].

I looked up Ellen White's uses of the word *miasma*. Most of them were metaphorical; only one, as I recall, would I be willing to see squarely through the "miasma theory" glasses, and I can't be certain that she had bought into the theory in full even then. We all use the language we have at our disposal to discuss matters, but the words mean what we make them mean. The fact that Mrs. White used the term *miasma* doesn't prove that she believed disease came from foul odors; she could be referring to other unhealthful conditions in low-lying places. But it does not discredit her if she did believe the theory for a time and later changed her mind as more information became available.

I wonder if the miasma issue might not be parallel in some sense to what Mrs. White said about salt. Some of the reformers of her day had labeled it a poison (which it is in large enough quantities) and forbidden its use. She wrote, "I use some salt, and always have, because from the light given me by God, this article, in the place of being deleterious, is actually essential for the blood. The whys and wherefores of this I know not, but I give you the instruction as it is given me" [*Counsels on Diet and Foods,* 344]. The counsel she gave was sound, but she did not know (was not shown) the "whys and wherefores." Might her counsel against living in the midst of rotting vegetable material also have been sound but not for the reasons she assumed it was (the "whys and where-fores")?

[The Ellen G. White Estate Web site contains three questions and responses on this subject, all involving the same people and all with the same—or very similar—title lines. You can find more helpful material there.]

Question 67:
Should we avoid chemotherapy and other modern medical treatments?
("Breast Cancer and Use of Herbs and Not Drugs")

A friend of mine has breast cancer, and a member of our church has told her that Mrs. White said we should use herbs and not drugs such as chemotherapy. Is this true? Are we not to use modern technology to attempt to control or eliminate cancer?

You have asked a question that is not easy to answer, at least in part. The part that *is* easy is your last question, about using modern technology to cure cancer. Mrs. White herself provides us an example here. She developed a cancerous spot on her forehead, and she had X-ray treatments for it, which killed the cancer. You will find her reference to this in *Selected Messages,* book 2, page 303, at the end of a chapter on "Ellen G. White's Use of Remedial Agencies."

On Mrs. White's references to drugs in general, it is helpful to know what her primary concerns were. Early in Mrs. White's ministry, the "big three" drugs that were widely used medically were opium, calomel, and nux vomica. You can read Mrs. White's comments about them in *Selected Messages,* book 2, pages 441–454. You probably recognize opium. Calomel is a compound of mercury, which today is treated as a hazardous material. Mrs. White described its effects in the pages I referred you to. The third, nux vomica, contains the poison strychnine. These were indeed "poisonous drugs," and physicians gave them in doses large or small.

Mrs. White's condemnation of the use of "poisonous drugs" appears most often, I think, in the context of seeking a cure for some temporary condition that the body would throw off by itself if it were given the proper rest, nutrition, exercise, air, and other support. The natural remedies are better than taking a dose of something in most such cases. But I, personally, am not willing to call all drugs poisonous just because Mrs. White referred to certain poisonous drugs. Our situation today is somewhat different from how things were then. With extensive scientific testing, the usefulness and safety of drugs is supposed to be established before they are made available to the general public.

The drugs used in chemotherapy are poisonous. The aim, as I understand it, is to give it in doses high enough to kill the cancer but low enough not to kill the patient. Though chemotherapy is no surefire cure for cancer, it does seem to have helped a good many people who would otherwise have died from their cancers. One important difference between these poisonous drugs and the ones Mrs. White wrote about is that these have actually been demonstrated to attack the problem—in this case, the cancer. Nineteenth-century doctors were trying to treat the symptoms, and even then, they had no idea what the drugs they gave actually did.

Are there viable alternatives to chemotherapy which are more in line with what Mrs. White called for? I remember hearing about the "grape cure" in my teens, but you almost never hear about it today. I am guessing this means that it didn't work in a high enough percentage of cases. I have had friends who tried alternative, "natural," or experimental cures. They are dead now. In examples like these, people must prayerfully, carefully, consider the options and do what they think is best.

Part 5

Questions About the Adventist Church

Question 68:
Did the leaders of the Adventist Church reject the 1888 message?
("The 1888 Message Rejected by SDA Leaders?")

Did Ellen White say that most of the leaders of the Seventh-day Adventist Church rejected the 1888 message that Jones and Waggoner preached?

I don't know of such a statement from Mrs. White's writings. I will copy for you portions of Arthur L. White's summary of this matter from *Ellen G. White: The Lonely Years 1876–1891,* volume 3 of his six-volume biography of Mrs. White (pages 394–397).

Minneapolis, and the ministerial institute that preceded it, brings to mind a matter of great importance—the message of righteousness by faith and the considerable resistance that met its presentation. . . . [C]ertain points of background and developments should be considered. . . .

5. . . . [T]here is very little by way of a day-by-day record, for the practice had not yet been adopted of reporting all meetings. . . .

7. As to establishing positions, no official action was taken in regard to the theological questions discussed. The uniform witness concerning the attitude toward the matter of righteousness by faith was that there were mixed reactions. These were described succinctly by [A. T.] Jones in 1893: "I know that some there accepted it; others rejected it entirely. . . . Others tried to stand halfway between, and get it that way."—GCB 1893, p. 185. Ellen White and others corroborate this. It is not possible to establish, from the records available, the relative number in each of the three groups.

8. The concept that the General Conference, and thus the denomination, rejected the message of righteousness by faith in 1888 is without foundation and was not projected until forty years after the Minneapolis meeting, and thirteen years after Ellen White's death. Contemporary records yield no suggestion of denominational rejection. There is no E. G. White statement anywhere that says this was so. The concept of such rejection has been put forward by individuals, none of whom were present at Minneapolis, and in the face of the witness of responsible men who were there. . . .

14. The Minneapolis session and its problems did not become a topic to which Ellen White would often refer. It was one event among others in her life experience. She was not obsessed with the matter. She did occasionally refer to the loss to individuals and the church because of the attitudes of certain ones there. To Ellen White it was a matter of picking up and pressing on, not losing sight of the vital truths reemphasized at the session.

Question 69:
Did Ellen White say the General Conference is Babylon?
("Did Ellen G. White Wrote That SDA General Conference is Babylon?")

> *A brother in Christ, with whom I correspond, is telling me that Mrs. White wrote that the Seventh-day Adventist General Conference is Babylon. He says that the proof is in the* General Conference Bulletin, *in a quote dated April 3, 1901: "That these men should stand in a sacred place, to be as the voice of God to the people, as we once believed the General Conference to be —that is past" (25).*
>
> *However, in things Mrs. White wrote after this date of April 3, 1901, I find a different view: "During the General Conference the Lord wrought mightily for His people. Every time I think of that meeting, a sweet solemnity comes over me, and sends a glow of gratitude to my soul. We have seen the stately steppings of the Lord our Redeemer. We praise His holy name, for He has brought deliverance to His people" (*Review and Herald, *November 26, 1901). Can you provide to me other quotes from Mrs. White that prove the Seventh-day Adventist Church will make it through to the end, including the General Conference?*

You've done some good homework! You found an important statement that provides a corrective to your friend's one-sided application of Mrs. White's other statement. You also did not accept the words that he put into Mrs. White's mouth—according to your account above, he claimed that she had said the General Conference was Babylon. But he didn't offer a statement that said that, did he? He couldn't, because there isn't one.

In 1901, after the General Conference session, Mrs. White wrote to her own son Edson, who was unhappy over some unjust treatment he had received at the hands of the Review and Herald Publishing Association prior to 1901. He was seeking compensation, and she reproved him: "It hurts me to think that you are using words which I wrote prior to the conference. Since the conference great changes have been made."—Letter 54, 1901 (To "My Dear Son Edson," J. E. White, June 1901) [*Manuscript Releases, 3:205*].

In 1905, she wrote of the church (which, of course, includes the General Conference) in a decidedly "non-Babylon" manner: "We cannot now step off the foundation that God has established. We cannot now enter into any new organization; for this would mean apostasy from the truth."—Manuscript 129, 1905 (*Selected Messages,* 2:390).

In 1909, in volume 9 of the *Testimonies,* Mrs. White published the following affirmation of confidence in the church and its broad based leadership, as had been established in that 1901 General Conference Session:

> I have often been instructed by the Lord that no man's judgment should be surrendered to the judgment of any other one man. Never should the mind of one man or the minds of a few men be regarded as sufficient in wisdom and power to control the work and to say what plans shall be followed. But when, in a General Conference, the judgment of the brethren assembled from all parts of the field is exercised, private independence and private judgment must not be stubbornly maintained, but surrendered. Never should a laborer regard as a virtue the persistent maintenance of his position of independence, contrary to the decision of the general body (260).

I think that is quite a direct answer to the claim that your friend made. It explains the meaning of her earlier statement, when the General Conference consisted of about three men who thought they could dictate to the whole church. This problem was resolved in 1901. Mrs. White's later statements, both immediately after the resolution (as in the statement you found) and much later (as I have noted above) show that she did not hold the view that the General Conference was Babylon.

In 1913, she wrote the following in a communication to the delegates at the General Conference session:

> When in the night season I am unable to sleep, I lift my heart in prayer to God, and He strengthens me, and gives me the assurance that He is with His ministering servants in the home field and in distant lands. I am encouraged and blessed as I realize that the God of Israel is still guiding His people, and that He will continue to be with them, even to the end (*Life Sketches of Ellen G. White,* 437, 438).

In *Testimonies to Ministers and Gospel Workers,* the entire first section gives Mrs. White's view on the question of whether the church is Babylon. Here is one section from it, from page 41:

> When anyone arises, either among us or outside of us, who is burdened with a message which declares that the people of God are numbered with Babylon, and claims that the loud cry is a call to come out of her, you may know that he is not bearing the message of truth. Receive him not, nor bid him Godspeed; for God has not spoken by him, neither has He given a message to him, but he has run before he was sent.

Though these passages from *Testimonies to Ministers and Gospel Workers* were written in 1893, we do not find Mrs. White repudiating them or contradicting them later on. In fact, they were written during the very time that she was keenly aware of the problems in leadership at the General Conference. She did not try to make a distinction, saying that it was wrong to declare the church to be Babylon but it was correct to declare the General Conference to be Babylon. No, for her it was one package—the church: enfeebled, defective, but still the one object upon earth on which God bestows His supreme regard.

See also the two following questions and answers.

Question 70:
Where did Ellen White say that God has left the church?
(" 'God Has Left the Church Long Ago' ")

I read an Ellen G. White quote that says, "God has left the church long ago." The source has escaped me, and I would like to get the context in which that quote applied.

Using some of the words you gave me, I did a search for such a statement. I did not find it. Actually, I have a hard time thinking that Mrs. White made a statement such as you have asked for. I recall other statements she made, with which this one would be quite out of harmony. Here's a prime one:

> During ages of spiritual darkness the church of God has been as a city set on a hill. From age to age, through successive generations, the pure doctrines of heaven have been unfolding within its borders. Enfeebled and defective as it may appear, the church is the one object upon which God bestows in a special sense His supreme regard. It is the theater of His grace, in which He delights to reveal His power to transform hearts (*The Acts of the Apostles*, 12).

If Mrs. White believed that God had left the church long ago, why would she stay with it?

It is possible that you may be thinking of a much more limited kind of statement, from the years between 1888 and 1901—the ones featured in A. V. Olson's book *Thirteen Crisis Years: 1888–1901*. Here are some statements along this line, as collected in the book *Last Day Events*, pages 50, 51:

> The voice from Battle Creek [the General Conference], which has been regarded as authority in counseling how the work should be done, is no longer the voice of God.—17MR 185 (1896). . . .
>
> That these men should stand in a sacred place, to be as the voice of God to the people, as we once believed the General Conference to be—that is past.—GCB April 3, 1901, p. 25.

You will find, however, that Mrs. White did not continue to hold such a negative view. After the reorganization of 1901 addressed the serious problems, she took quite a different view. Here are several statements that she made after that reorganization (all found in *Last Day Events,* 55, 56). The last quotation is her final message to the Seventh-day Adventist Church in General Conference session, read to the assembly by the General Conference president, A. G. Daniells, on May 27, 1913:

We cannot now step off the foundation that God has established. We cannot now enter into any new organization, for this would mean apostasy from the truth.—2SM 390 (1905).

I am instructed to say to Seventh-day Adventists the world over, God has called us as a people to be a peculiar treasure unto Himself. He has appointed that His church on earth shall stand perfectly united in the Spirit and counsel of the Lord of hosts to the end of time. —2SM 397 (1908).

At times, when a small group of men entrusted with the general management of the work have, in the name of the General Conference, sought to carry out unwise plans to restrict God's work, I have said that I could no longer regard the voice of the General Conference, represented by these few men, as the voice of God. But this is not saying that the decisions of a General Conference composed of an assembly of duly appointed, representative men from all parts of the field should not be respected.

God has ordained that the representatives of His church from all parts of the earth, when assembled in a General Conference, shall have authority. The error that some are in danger of committing is in giving to the mind and judgment of one man, or of a small group of men, the full measure of authority and influence that God has invested in His church in the judgment and voice of the General Conference assembled to plan for the prosperity and advancement of His work.—9T 260, 261 (1909).

God has invested His church with special authority and power which no one can be justified in disregarding and despising, for he who does this despises the voice of God.—AA 164 (1911).

I am encouraged and blessed as I realize that the God of Israel is still guiding His people and that He will continue to be with them, even to the end.—2SM 406 (1913).

If you will read the entire chapter of *Last Day Events*, you will see the whole sweep of the issue and get a good overview of the reasons why Mrs. White said what she did and why she was later able to say something quite different.

See also the preceding and the following questions and answers.

Question 71:
Will another church replace the Adventist Church?
("Should We Look for Another Church?")

> *Where can I find the reference to the phrase "should we look for an-other church"? Mrs. White either was in vision or speaking to the Lord or an angel in the later part of her years and seemed to be asking if there would be another group who would be given the message.*

I did a computer search for the phrase "look for another church" and came up with nothing. But your inquiry reminded me of a statement from Mrs. White, found in *Selected Messages,* book 1, page 179:

> You will take passages in the *Testimonies* that speak of the close of probation, of the shaking among God's people, and you will talk of a coming out from this people of a purer, holier people that will arise. Now all this pleases the enemy. We should not needlessly take a course that will make differences or create dissension. We should not give the impression that if our particular ideas are not followed, it is because the ministers are lacking in comprehension and in faith, and are walking in darkness.

In a similar vein, she wrote,

> Satan will work his miracles to deceive; he will set up his power as supreme. The church may appear as about to fall, but it does not fall. It remains, while the sinners in Zion will be sifted out—the chaff separated from the precious wheat. This is a terrible ordeal, but never-theless it must take place. None but those who have been overcoming by the blood of the Lamb and the word of their testimony will be found with the loyal and true, without spot or stain of sin, without guile in their mouths. We must be divested of our self-righteousness and arrayed in the righteousness of Christ (*Selected Messages,* 2:380).

I cannot be certain that there is no statement from Mrs. White along the lines you have asked for (though evidently not with just those words), but I was not successful in finding one. Perhaps one of the statements I gave you will meet the need. I hope so.

See also the two preceding questions and answers.

Question 72:
Did Mrs. White say the Adventist Church "will go through"?
("The Church Will Go Through")

I am looking for references for Mrs. White's comment that "the church will go through." Is she referring specifically to the Seventh-day Adventist Church or the church in general?

When I think of Mrs. White's comments along these lines, I think of her statement that it will appear that the church is about to fall, but it does not fall; it remains. I'll quote it for you here, with the paragraph before it for context:

> We are to be ready and waiting for the orders of God. Nations will be stirred to their very center. Support will be withdrawn from those who proclaim God's only standard of righteousness, the only sure test of character. And all who will not bow to the decree of the national councils and obey the national laws to exalt the sabbath instituted by the man of sin, to the disregard of God's holy day, will feel, not the oppressive power of popery alone, but of the Protestant world, the image of the beast.
>
> Satan will work his miracles to deceive; he will set up his power as supreme. The church may appear as about to fall, but it does not fall. It remains, while the sinners in Zion will be sifted out—the chaff separated from the precious wheat. This is a terrible ordeal, but nevertheless it must take place. None but those who have been overcoming by the blood of the Lamb and the word of their testimony will be found with the loyal and true, without spot or stain of sin, without guile in their mouths. We must be divested of our self-righteousness and arrayed in the righteousness of Christ (*Selected Messages,* 2:380).

In this statement, it should be clear that she has in mind the church that keeps the commandments of God.

Question 73:
Shouldn't we be preaching the Adventist "pillars"?
("The Mission")

You folks need to get back to the basics. Remember, we are called to be a peculiar nation. We are called to give the trumpet a certain sound. We were called to come out of Babylon and preach the truths for our day if we really want Christ to come back. We are starting to preach just like all the other churches.

I used to be a Catholic, and I learned and accepted the three angels' messages, the sanctuary, the Sabbath, and the message about the identity of the beast and the image of the beast. I know these messages are the pillars of this church. Why are we not putting them in newspapers and magazines, on the radio and on billboards, etc., as the Spirit of Prophecy said?

I think we are on the same wavelength regarding the importance of the distinctive message Seventh-day Adventists have for this world in the last days. However, we also have counsel from Mrs. White regarding how to go about our work. She cautioned us not to lead with the things that separate us from other Christians. Here are a couple paragraphs from *Evangelism*, pages 200, 201:

> In laboring in a new field, do not think it your duty to say at once to the people, We are Seventh-day Adventists; we believe that the seventh day is the Sabbath; we believe in the nonimmortality of the soul. This would often erect a formidable barrier between you and those you wish to reach. Speak to them, as you have opportunity, upon points of doctrine on which you can agree. Dwell on the necessity of practical godliness. Give them evidence that you are a Christian, desiring peace, and that you love their souls. Let them see that you are conscientious. Thus you will gain their confidence; and there will be time enough for doctrines. Let the heart be won, the soil prepared, and then sow the seed, presenting in love the truth as it is in Jesus.—*Gospel Workers*, pp. 119, 120. (1915)

Guard Against Closing the Listeners' Ears.—Last night in my sleeping hours I seemed to be in meeting with my brethren, listening to One who spoke as having authority. He said: "Many souls will attend this meeting who are honestly ignorant of the truths which will be presented before them. They will listen and become interested, because Christ is drawing them. . . . The greatest care is needed in dealing with these souls. Do not at the outset press before the people the most objectionable features of our faith, lest you close their ears to which these things come as a new revelation. Let such portions of truth be dealt out to them as they may be able to grasp and appreciate; though it should appear strange and startling, many will recognize with joy the new light that is shed on the Word of God, whereas if truth were presented in so large a measure that they could not receive it, some would go away, and never come again. More than this, they would misrepresent the truth."—*General Conference Bulletin*, Feb. 25, 1895.

Question 74:
What did Ellen White say about women preaching?
("Women Should not Be Speaking in Church?")

In our church today we had one of our women speaking, and it was a good sermon. But as soon as the service was over, I got a note that said women should not be speaking in church. The note referenced 1 Timothy 2:11–15 and 1 Corinthians 14:33–35.

In the days in which Mrs. White began her ministry and through a good portion of her ministry, many people in the general society of the United States felt that it was improper, unladylike, for a woman to speak in public. The issue was not so much preaching but speaking *at all* in public. Among the substantial part of the populace that professed to believe and follow the Bible, many took Paul's counsel in such verses as 1 Corinthians 14:34 and 1 Timothy 2:11, 12 as forbidding women to speak in church.

Neither Mrs. White nor our other pioneers upheld such a view. From time to time, the *Review and Herald* of the 1850s and on through the 1890s, and *Signs of the Times* after it came along, would carry articles addressing the issue by the title "May Women Speak in Church?" or something similar. Their answer always was Yes. When I first saw these articles, I thought that our pioneers were writing in this manner to defend Mrs. White's ministry. I soon came to the realization that they were not—they were defending the right of *any* woman to testify or otherwise participate orally in the services of the church.

By her example and by a few specific counsels, Mrs. White encouraged women to speak publicly. This is not the same as saying that she encouraged them to seek the position of minister or elder, for I do not find her doing so. But she believed—and acted on this belief in her own life—that women had a contribution to make to the work of God, and that this might legitimately involve speaking in church—even preaching.

Mrs. White never occupied the pulpit on Sabbath morning if her husband, James, was there and available. He would preach in the morning, and she would speak in the afternoon. After his death, though, she did accept invitations to preach on Sabbath morning. But she did so not as a minister or preacher but as—to use her own preferred designation for herself—a "messenger of the Lord."

Mrs. White herself wrote once of an objection that was circulated against her public speaking.

> I had in the evening, it was stated, the largest congregation that had ever assembled at Arbuckle. The house was full. Many came from five to ten and twelve miles. The Lord gave me special power in speaking. The congregation listened as if spellbound. Not one left the house although I talked above one hour. Before I commenced talking, Elder Haskell had a bit of paper that was handed in, quoting certain texts prohibiting women speaking in public. He took up the matter in a brief manner and very clearly expressed the meaning of the apostle's words.—Letter 17a, 1880, page 2. (Written from Oakland, California, April 1, 1880, to James White.) [*Manuscript Releases,* 10:70].

I think the key thing for someone like your friend to see is that the Bible permits—even encourages—women to do certain kinds of speaking in the church, so the other texts cannot be blanket prohibitions. In that case, we can examine what Scripture says to find out what kind of speaking it approves of and what is out of harmony with it.

Question 75:
Should we keep the Old Testament feasts today?
("Observance of the Feasts Today?")

Is there anything in the writings of E. G. White either pro or con regarding the observance of the Old Testament feasts today? I am really confused on this issue—any suggestions?

I find nothing in Mrs. White's writings to support the idea that Christians should observe the feasts today. She herself did not observe them.

One statement that is often quoted in support of keeping the feasts is this one, from the *Review and Herald,* November 17, 1885:

> Well would it be for us to have a feast of tabernacles, a joyous commemoration of the blessings of God to us as a people. As the children of Israel celebrated the deliverance that God wrought for their fathers, and his miraculous preservation of them during their journeyings from Egypt to the promised land, so should the people of God at the present time gratefully call to mind the various ways he has devised to bring them out from the world, out from the darkness of error, into the precious light of truth. We should often bring to remembrance the dependence upon God of those who first led out in this work. We should gratefully regard the old way-marks, and refresh our souls with memories of the loving-kindness of our gracious Benefactor.

When Mrs. White calls for "*a* feast of tabernacles" rather than "*the* Feast of Tabernacles," she seems to be asking us to do something similar to—but not the same as—what Israel of old did. In the remainder of the paragraph, she describes the elements that she was calling for. These elements do not require our observance of the Feast of Tabernacles as such. In fact, in this statement Mrs. White appears to call for something more frequent than the annual feast: "We should *often* bring to remembrance . . ."

On occasion Mrs. White seems to have compared our camp meetings to the Feast of Tabernacles:

The forces of the enemies are strengthening, and as a people we are misrepresented; but shall we not gather our forces together, and come up to the feast of tabernacles? Let us not treat this matter as one of little importance, but let the army of the Lord be on the ground to represent the work and cause of God in Australia. Let no one plead an excuse at such a time. One of the reasons why we have appointed the camp-meeting to be held at Melbourne, is that we desire the people of that vicinity to become acquainted with our doctrines and works. We want them to know what we are, and what we believe. Let every one pray, and make God his trust. Those who are barricaded with prejudice must hear the warning message for this time. We must find our way to the hearts of the people. Therefore come to the camp-meeting, even though you have to make a sacrifice to do so, and the Lord will bless your efforts to honour his cause and advance his work (*Bible Echo and Signs of the Times,* December 8, 1893).

In the remainder of the article from which I just quoted, Mrs. White gives many reasons for people to attend the camp meeting but observing the Bible feast is not one of them.

You asked whether there was anything "pro or con" in Mrs. White's writings about keeping the feasts. It seems to me that the following statement says that the Passover has been replaced by the Lord's Supper. See what you think.

Christ was standing at the point of transition between two economies and their two great festivals. He, the spotless Lamb of God, was about to present Himself as a sin offering, that He would thus bring to an end the system of types and ceremonies that for four thousand years had pointed to His death. As He ate the Passover with His disciples, He instituted in its place the service that was to be the memorial of His great sacrifice. The national festival of the Jews was to pass away forever. The service which Christ established was to be observed by His followers in all lands and through all ages (*The Desire of Ages,* 652).

Mrs. White wrote that in the Last Supper and His crucifixion to follow, Jesus would "bring to an end the system of types and ceremonies that for four thousand years had pointed to His death." She added that Jesus instituted the Lord's Supper in place of the Passover. On these bases, I personally feel that agitation about keeping the feasts is not appropriate and may in fact be a distraction, a sidetrack, for God's people today.

Question 76:
Did Ellen White warn against having large churches?
("Any Counsel Regarding Church Size?")

Did Ellen White counsel against large churches? I've heard people say this, but I can't find this thought in your search engine.

Yes, Mrs. White did have certain words of warning and counsel regarding large churches. I'll quote a couple paragraphs for you below, but for more information I'll refer you to the three-volume index to Mrs. White's books. Under the heading "Churches," section number 7 is entitled "Large." The quotations that follow come from this section, and the index can refer you to many more. About one whole column of references there concerns this subject. If you don't have the index yourself, you may know someone who does. Or use the search capability on our Web site to search for "large churches" or "large church." You will likely get more hits than you will find in the index, but a number of them will probably not be dealing with the issues you are interested in, and you may miss some other statements the index includes because they don't happen to use the exact expression "large church" or "large churches."

> Our duty to act as missionaries for God in the very position where He has placed us has been greatly overlooked by us as a people. Many are eagerly turning from present duties and opportunities to some wider field; many imagine that in some other position they would find it less difficult to obey the truth. Our larger churches are looked upon as enjoying great advantages, and there is among our people a growing tendency to leave their special post of duty and move to Battle Creek or to the vicinity of some other large church. This practice not only threatens the prosperity and even the life of our smaller churches, but it is preventing us from doing the very work which God has given us to do, and is destroying our spirituality and usefulness as a people (*Testimonies for the Church,* 5:184).

> Many of the members of our large churches are doing comparatively

nothing. They might accomplish a good work if, instead of crowding together, they would scatter into places that have not yet been entered by the truth. Trees that are planted too thickly do not flourish. They are transplanted by the gardener, that they may have room to grow and not become dwarfed and sickly. The same rule would work well for our large churches. Many of the members are dying spiritually for want of this very work. They are becoming sickly and inefficient. Transplanted, they would have room to grow strong and vigorous. It is not the purpose of God that His people should colonize or settle together in large communities. The disciples of Christ are His representatives upon the earth, and God designs that they shall be scattered all over the country, in the towns, cities, and villages, as lights amidst the darkness of the world. They are to be missionaries for God, by their faith and works testifying to the near approach of the coming Saviour (*Testimonies for the Church*, 8:244).

Part 6

Questions About Marriage and Sex

Question 77:
Should an Adventist marry only another Adventist?
("Views on Who One Should Marry of Miss White")

> *I am a Seventh-day Adventist in Malawi. I enjoy very much reading the spiritually enriching Ellen White literature. I have been closely follow-ing her writings in the books of hers that I have had a chance to read. However, I have not been able to get her opinion regarding marriage. If you have any information from her that points out her stand with regard to who a church member should marry, I would be very glad to have it. Here there is emphasis on marriage among church members (Seventh-day Adventists) only. I just want to have her stand on this issue.*

I had occasion to answer an inquiry similar to yours several months ago. In my reply I quoted from *Testimonies for the Church*, volume 5, chapter 43, "Marriage With Unbelievers"—a very helpful chapter. The inquirer asked not only about whether an Adventist should marry a non-Adventist, but also what constitutes an unbeliever. On that occasion I wrote the following:

To Mrs. White, what constitutes an unbeliever? Is it someone who does not believe the Christian message at all, or might it also apply to someone who has adopted the Christian faith but not the Adventist message?

It turns out that Mrs. White addressed this very question:

> Though the companion of your choice were in all other respects worthy (which he is not), yet he has not accepted the truth for this time; he is an unbeliever, and you are forbidden of heaven to unite yourself with him. You cannot, without peril to your soul, disregard this divine injunction (*Testimonies for the Church,* 5:364).

According to this statement, someone who "has not accepted the truth for this time" (an expression Mrs. White used for the Adventist message) is an unbeliever, one with whom we should not unite our lives. How can one who believes that Jesus is coming soon and who believes we have a world to warn and to win to the distinctive, last-day message of Seventh-day Adventists unite in life's strongest tie with someone who does not share that passion? When you think about it in that light, it really does not make sense to marry someone who doesn't share our convictions and mission.

What is the church's stand on its ministers marrying an Adventist to a non-Adventist? *The Church Manual* says, "The Seventh-day Adventist Church strongly discourages marriage between a Seventh-day Adventist and a non-Seventh-day Adventist, and strongly urges Seventh-day Adventist ministers not to perform such weddings" (2005 ed., 183).

The *Seventh-day Adventist Minister's Handbook* agrees, devoting nearly two pages to these matters. On the specific point of the minister's performing the ceremony, it concludes, "If a member chooses a partner who is not a member of the Church, the Church hopes that the couple will realize and appreciate that the Seventh-day Adventist pastor, who has covenanted to uphold the principles outlined above, should not be expected to perform such a marriage" (1997 ed., 261).

Question 78:
What did Ellen White say about sex in marriage?
("Sex in Marriage")

> *I am a Seventh-day Adventist in good and regular standing and a believer in the prophetic gift of Ellen G. White. I'm wondering whether anyone from the White Estate has attempted to interpret what Mrs. White meant by her comments on the subject of sex in marriage. It seems clear to me that she didn't teach it was only for the purpose of procreation.*

This is my understanding as well.

> *What are the "multitude of sins practiced in the marriage relation"? Frequency? Perversions? Both?*

I can only guess, but that guess would be "both." Excessive frequency increased the risk of pregnancy, and Mrs. White believed that having a great many children was not healthful physically or, in some respects, spiritually (tied down to home, reduced chance to witness, and even to feed one's own spiritual needs, etc.). She may also have been concerned about female diseases being caused or encouraged by frequent sexual relations. This may have been related to the difficulty of keeping clean in locations where good facilities for doing so were rare. This might be the cause of what she referred to as wearing out the female organs.

> *What would be considered a perversion?*

I don't know that Mrs. White ever explained what she may have had in mind along this line. I believe she would call excessive frequency a perversion. But she seems to have had other concerns in mind as well. We can only guess what they might have been. Sadomasochism? Sodomy? Whatever they were, she seems to have objected on the grounds that they were corrupting—morally perverse.

> *Some of the Seventh-day Adventist literature I have read does not take*

a strong stance on any style of sexual behavior in marriage as being sinful. All I want to know is what the Lord really says on the matter. I don't want to misinterpret what the Spirit of Prophecy says by falling short of God's ideals or raising an unreasonable standard.

This is a worthy goal. But if you are looking for someone—even Mrs. White—to tell you definitively what is approved and what is not, you may be disappointed. Or you may find someone to tell you—someone who has no more authority than you or the next person. You may need to work this out between you and the Lord in prayer and on the basis of larger principles.

God created sex. But just as we may take His good gifts of food and over-indulge in them, so may we misuse this gift. However, we may also obsess in the other direction, trying to be too careful. In the food arena, such obsessions may manifest themselves as anorexia or even as a "salvation by strictness in diet" mentality. Similarly, one may become so fixated on trying to resolve all these questions about sex that one forgets that God wants His married children to show love and tenderness to each other, including in their sexual relations. They should be concerned with honoring, building up, and ministering to the joys and needs of the other, in harmony with honoring God. Beyond these basics, I don't feel qualified to tell another what Mrs. White meant or precisely what their duty may be in these matters.

Question 79:
Can we use artificial birth control?
("Natural Birth Control vs. Other Means")

I am getting married and have been praying and searching in the Bible and Ellen G. White's writings about the issue of natural birth control versus other means. I am interested in knowing what knowledge people had in Mrs. White's day about fertility. She wrote,

> *In sending missionaries to distant countries, those men should be selected who know to economize, who have not large families, and who, realizing the shortness of time and the great work to be accomplished, will not fill their hands and houses with children, but will keep themselves as free as possible from everything that will divert their minds from their one great work. The wife, if devoted and left free to do so, can, by standing by the side of her husband, accomplish as much as he. God has blessed woman with talents to be used to His glory in bringing many sons and daughters to God; but many who might be efficient laborers are kept at home to care for their little ones (The Adventist Home, 165, 166).*

From this statement, it sounds like couples have a choice regarding whether or not to have children. Did couples know what time of month was best for avoiding pregnancy, or did they just abstain until a pregnancy would be OK?

Basically, the issue here is that Mrs. White says *what* but not *how*—isn't that right? She is clearly in favor of planning for children and controlling the number of children one has. She doesn't discuss how to accomplish this. She seems to assume that people know how it is done. I don't get the impression from her writings that she recommended that married couples have no sex until they desired to have a child. Rather, it seems to me that she urged that they exercise self-control in the frequency and timing of their relations in order to carry out the plans that they had made for a family. If this is correct, it corresponds to what is called the rhythm method today. I don't have specific information about when this was developed, but I would be surprised if its outlines were not widely known in the nineteenth century.

Seventh-day Adventists do not share the Catholic idea that sexual relations must always have the potential for conception nor that God has souls He intends to put into bodies and that artificial birth control frustrates His intentions. We believe that the sexual relationship is for relationship as well as procreation and that one may legitimately cultivate that relationship while exercising options to postpone parenthood. This is, of course, a personal matter, and I don't claim to speak for every Seventh-day Adventist. But our theology does not direct us to the same view the Catholics hold, and I think that most Seventh-day Adventists do not limit themselves to the rhythm method if other methods are within their reach.

I think that what is important to you is not so much what knowledge nineteenth-century people had, but what is a legitimate stance on these matters before God. I find no prohibition of birth control in Mrs. White's writings, whether by rhythm or by other means. I find there instead a level-headed, sensible approach to the matter of family planning that has the potential to maximize one's care for the children one does bring into the world and to enable maximum service for the Lord as well.

Question 80:
May divorced Adventists who have repented remarry?
("Divorce and Remarriage")

> *I am the head elder of a church. I have a very sticky situation, and I need some help as to how to proceed. There is a young divorced man in the church. He was responsible for the failure of his marriage because of his own infidelity. However, this was before he changed his life and accepted the Lord Jesus. He has since been baptized.*
>
> *This man has become enamored with a lovely girl who has grown up in the church. She is twenty-one years old. Her parents are not happy with this turn of events because he has two children. His wife is still alive and has not remarried.*
>
> *Did Mrs. White write anything about divorced individuals who have repented? Is the divorced individual condemned to solitude? What can I do?*

I am always reluctant to answer inquiries like this one because the situations are highly charged and I frequently don't feel that I know with certainty how to make them better. If people would simply live up to their promises and determine to do nothing in any line that would displease God or bring discredit on His work here on earth, they would avoid many of these vexing problems. But they do not.

You will find Mrs. White's comments on these matters primarily in three sources: *The Adventist Home,* pages 326–347; *Thoughts From the Mount of Blessing,* pages 63–65; and *Testimonies on Sexual Behavior, Adultery, and Divorce.* The sweep of her general counsel is found in the first two, while the third book deals in more detail with certain situations. I recommend them all to you.

In answer to your question at the end, let me quote a part of Mrs. White's general counsel as it appears in *The Adventist Home* and *Thoughts From the Mount of Blessing* and is quoted in *Testimonies on Sexual Behavior:*

> A woman may be legally divorced from her husband by the laws of the land and yet not divorced in the sight of God and according to the

higher law. There is only one sin, which is adultery, which can place the husband or wife in a position where they can be free from the marriage vow in the sight of God. Although the laws of the land may grant a divorce, yet they are husband and wife still in the Bible light, according to the laws of God.

I saw that Sister ——, as yet, has no right to marry another man; but if she, or any other woman, should obtain a divorce legally on the ground that her husband was guilty of adultery, then she is free to be married to whom she chooses (*The Adventist Home*, 344; *Testimonies on Sexual Behavior*, 78, 79).

Among the Jews a man was permitted to put away his wife for the most trivial offenses, and the woman was then at liberty to marry again. This practice led to great wretchedness and sin. In the Sermon on the Mount Jesus declared plainly that there could be no dissolution of the marriage tie except for unfaithfulness to the marriage vow. "Everyone," He said, "that putteth away his wife, saving for the cause of fornication, maketh her an adulteress: and whosoever shall marry her when she is put away committeth adultery" [Matt. 5:32, R.V.].

When the Pharisees afterward questioned Him concerning the lawfulness of divorce, Jesus pointed His hearers back to the marriage institution as ordained at creation. "Because of the hardness of your hearts," He said, Moses "suffered you to put away your wives: but from the beginning it was not so" (Matt. 19:8). . . . As the Creator joined the hands of the holy pair in wedlock, saying, a man shall "leave his father and his mother, and shall cleave unto his wife: and they shall be one" (Gen. 2:24), He enunciated the law of marriage for all the children of Adam to the close of time (*Testimonies on Sexual Behavior*, 79, 80).

You asked specifically about the person who has repented. If one has repented, it means he has accepted God's view of his error, has confessed the error, and has done all he can to make matters right. True repentance will result in one's seeking to know God's instruction for moving forward as well. It was disregard of God's instructions that caused the breakup of the first marriage. Will disregard of His instructions provide a solid foundation for a second marriage?

In our age that gives priority to feelings, sympathy for one in "solitude" may run strong, but it does not alter the commands of Jesus. Our only safety is in obedience, not in following inclination, no matter how the flesh may clamor. God will give grace for holy living if we determine to obey Him and trust Him. This is how I see it. I invite you to read the Bible for yourself on the matter and also to review the comments of Mrs. White.

Part 7

Questions About Spiritual Life

Question 81:
Did Ellen White say we can't know whether we're saved?
("Salvation")

What was Sister White's response to people's claim, "I know I am saved"? Also her response to once saved, always saved?

Ellen White did write, "Those who accept the Saviour, however sincere their conversion, should never be taught to say or to feel that they are saved" (*Christ's Object Lessons,* 155). However, a closer look at her cautions regarding this subject reveals that, in context, she wasn't speaking against the certainty of a believer's present standing with God. Instead, she was warning against the presumptuous "once saved, always saved" teaching of eternal security—against claiming "I am saved" while continuing to transgress the law of God. Here is her full statement:

> Peter's fall was not instantaneous, but gradual. Self-confidence led him to the belief that he was saved, and step after step was taken in the downward path, until he could deny his Master. Never can we safely put confidence in self or feel, this side of heaven, that we are secure

against temptation. Those who accept the Saviour, however sincere their conversion, should never be taught to say or to feel that they are saved. This is misleading. Everyone should be taught to cherish hope and faith; but even when we give ourselves to Christ and know that He accepts us, we are not beyond the reach of temptation. God's Word declares, "Many shall be purified, and made white, and tried" (Dan. 12:10). Only he who endures the trial will receive the crown of life (James 1:12) (*Christ's Object Lessons,* 155, emphasis added).

That Ellen White understood the proper basis for true Christian assurance is evidenced by the following remark she made before the church's General Conference session: "Each one of you may know for yourself that you have a living Saviour, that He is your helper and your God. You need not stand where you say, 'I do not know whether I am saved.' Do you believe in Christ as your personal Saviour? If you do, then rejoice" (*The General Conference Bulletin,* April 10, 1901).

To a woman who was struggling with doubts, Ellen White wrote,

> The message from God to me for you is "Him that cometh unto me, I will in no wise cast out" (John 6:37). If you have nothing else to plead before God but this one promise from your Lord and Saviour, you have the assurance that you will never, never be turned away. It may seem to you that you are hanging upon a single promise, but appropriate that one promise, and it will open to you the whole treasure house of the riches of the grace of Christ. Cling to that promise and you are safe. "Him that cometh unto me, I will in no wise cast out." Present this assurance to Jesus, and you are as safe as though inside the city of God (*Manuscript Releases,* 10:175).

So there you have the more complete picture. Mrs. White did advise against a "once saved, always saved" viewpoint. But she knew how to present a biblical assurance to those plagued with doubt.

Question 82:
How can Christians best resolve conflicts?
("Ellen White Quotes on Solving Conflict by Discussion?")

> *I need some quotes on what Ellen White says about how discussion can solve conflicts. This is for a school project, but I would definitely use the information for life.*

The passage below may be useful to you. It is from *Patriarchs and Prophets*, pages 519, 520. You may want to go back and read the part of the story that comes before this to get the whole picture.

You may also find a chapter in *Gospel Workers* helpful (498–502). It's about how to resolve conflicts and misunderstandings and hurts in the church. Basically, Mrs. White's counsel was to follow Jesus' instructions in Matthew 18. Here's the material from *Patriarchs and Prophets*:

How often serious difficulties arise from a simple misunderstanding, even among those who are actuated by the worthiest motives; and without the exercise of courtesy and forbearance, what serious and even fatal results may follow. The ten tribes remembered how, in Achan's case, God had rebuked the lack of vigilance to discover the sins existing among them. Now they resolved to act promptly and earnestly; but in seeking to shun their first error, they had gone to the opposite extreme. Instead of making courteous inquiry to learn the facts in the case, they had met their brethren with censure and condemnation. Had the men of Gad and Reuben retorted in the same spirit, war would have been the result. While it is important on the one hand that laxness in dealing with sin be avoided, it is equally important on the other to shun harsh judgment and groundless suspicion.

While very sensitive to the least blame in regard to their own course, many are too severe in dealing with those whom they suppose to be in error. No one was ever reclaimed from a wrong position by censure and reproach; but many are thus driven further from the right path and led to harden their hearts against conviction. A spirit of kindness, a courteous, forbearing deportment may save the erring and hide a multitude of sins.

The wisdom displayed by the Reubenites and their companions is worthy of imitation. While honestly seeking to promote the cause of true religion, they were misjudged and severely censured, yet they manifested no resentment. They listened with courtesy and patience to the charges of their brethren before attempting to make their defense, and then fully explained their motives and showed their innocence. Thus the difficulty which had threatened such serious consequences was amicably settled.

Even under false accusation those who are in the right can afford to be calm and considerate. God is acquainted with all that is misunderstood and misinterpreted by men, and we can safely leave our case in His hands. He will as surely vindicate the cause of those who put their trust in Him as He searched out the guilt of Achan. Those who are actuated by the spirit of Christ will possess that charity which suffers long and is kind.

It is the will of God that union and brotherly love should exist among His people. The prayer of Christ just before His crucifixion was that His disciples might be one as He is one with the Father, that the world might believe that God had sent Him. This most touching and wonderful prayer reaches down the ages, even to our day; for His words were, "Neither pray I for these alone, but for them also which shall believe on Me through their word." John 17:20. While we are not to sacrifice one principle of truth, it should be our constant aim to reach this state of unity. This is the evidence of our discipleship. Said Jesus, "By this shall all men know that ye are My disciples, if ye have love one to another." John 13:35. The apostle Peter exhorts the church, "Be ye all of one mind, having compassion one of another; love as brethren, be pitiful, be courteous: not rendering evil for evil, or railing for railing: but contrariwise blessing; knowing that ye are thereunto called, that ye should inherit a blessing." 1 Peter 3:8, 9.

Question 83:
Does what other people think matter?
("Sexual Relations")

> *I am currently having a strong debate with another Adventist who is living with his girlfriend and refuses to accept anything that I say to him about his actions being wrong. He says he is not having a sexual relationship with her, they live in separate rooms, and he doesn't care that other people may think he is doing something wrong. His attitude is that he knows and God knows what the situation is, and everyone else with their "depraved" minds can think what they like about his situation because he is not violating anything in the Bible.*
>
> *Has Mrs. White written anything on this topic? I know he is a reader and reads many of her books, and if he reads it for himself, he won't be able to make any more excuses.*

The Bible itself tells us, "Abstain from all appearance of evil" (1 Thessalonians 5:22, KJV). Jesus said, "Let your light so shine before men, that they may see your good works, and glorify your Father which is in heaven" (Matthew 5:16, KJV). I do not see that this arrangement contributes to the glory of God. Your friend may thumb his nose at the world, charging that those who challenge him have "depraved" minds, but the fact is that essentially everyone—Christian and non-Christian alike—will assume that they are having sexual relations. In my view, the damage to his reputation is not worth whatever benefit he may think is there. Further, by maintaining this arrangement, he is damaging his girlfriend's reputation, for people will assume the same of her that they do of him. He should take godly initiative in this matter to bring it to an end for both their sakes—and especially so if he regards her as his girlfriend. He should be seeking to guard her reputation even more than his own.

Here are a couple statements from Mrs. White that might apply.

> It is not enough for you to avoid the appearance of evil; you must go farther than this; you must "learn to do well." You must represent Christ to the world. It must be your daily study how you can learn to

work the works of God. His followers are to be living epistles, "known and read of all men" (*Messages to Young People,* 348). [What are people "reading" in the epistle of this man's life now?]

It is important that children and youth should be trained to guard their words and deeds; for their course of action causes sunshine or shadow, not only in their own home, but also with all with whom they come in contact. But before the youth can be careful and thoughtful and refrain from every appearance of evil, they must have that wisdom which comes from above, and the strength which Jesus alone can impart (*Messages to Young People,* 345).

Question 84:
What is the sin against the Holy Spirit?
("Ellen G. White on Sin Against Holy Ghost")

What is the sin against the Holy Ghost all about? How can I be sure that I have not committed the sin against the Holy Ghost? Why can this particular sin not be forgiven?

Following my answer I will copy for you a couple of paragraphs from *The Desire of Ages* in which Mrs. White addressed the questions you have asked. (These paragraphs come from pages 321–323. You would find the whole passage, through page 325, enlightening.) You will see that she presents this sin as the resisting of the Holy Spirit's call to us to repent and turn to God. Even in the face of the strongest evidence and appeals, we are free, if we wish, to refuse to yield to God. If we continually resist, eventually we won't be impressed at all by the Spirit's most powerful work on our behalf. We will have placed ourselves beyond God's reach because He will not violate our will. God cannot forgive this sin because we refuse to bring it to Him or even to listen to His pleadings.

How can we know that we have not committed this sin? If we still feel the call of God to yield our life to Him, that is the work of the Holy Spirit on our heart. If we have been resisting His call, we can be thankful that He is still working on us, and *we must not delay*! We must make a full surrender of our life to the One who died for us. As He held nothing back, so we must hold nothing back. Delay or refusal is dangerous. *Now* is the accepted hour, the Bible says; *now* is the day of salvation.

It was just before this that Jesus had a second time performed the miracle of healing a man possessed, blind and dumb, and the Pharisees had reiterated the charge, "He casteth out devils through the prince of the devils." Matt. 9:34. Christ told them plainly that in attributing the work of the Holy Spirit to Satan, they were cutting themselves off from the fountain of blessing. Those who had spoken against Jesus Himself, not discerning His divine character, might receive forgiveness; for through the Holy Spirit they might be brought to see their error and repent. Whatever the sin, if the soul repents and believes, the guilt is washed away in the blood of Christ; but he who rejects the work of the Holy Spirit is placing himself where repentance and faith cannot come to him. It is by the Spirit that God works upon the hearts when men willfully reject the Spirit, and declare It to be from Satan, they cut off the channel by which God can communicate with them. When the Spirit is finally rejected, there is no more that God can do for the soul. . . .

It is not God that blinds the eyes of men or hardens their hearts. He sends them light to correct their errors, and to lead them in safe paths; it is by the rejection of this light that the eyes are blinded and the heart hardened. Often the process is gradual, and almost imperceptible. Light comes to the soul through God's word, through His servants, or by the direct agency of His Spirit; but when one ray of light is disregarded, there is a partial benumbing of the spiritual perceptions, and the second revealing of light is less clearly discerned. So the darkness increases, until it is night in the soul. Thus it had been with these Jewish leaders. They were convinced that a divine power attended Christ, but in order to resist the truth, they attributed the work of the Holy Spirit to Satan. In doing this they deliberately chose deception; they yielded themselves to Satan, and henceforth they were controlled by his power.

Question 85:
Can Satan read our minds?
("Can Satan Read Our Minds?")

Can Satan read our minds?

Mrs. White wrote,

Satan cannot read our thoughts, but he can see our actions, hear our words; and from his long knowledge of the human family, he can shape his temptations to take advantage of our weak points of character. And how often do we let him into the secret of how he may obtain the victory over us. Oh, that we might control our words and actions! How strong we would become if our words were of such an order that we would not be ashamed to meet the record of them in the day of judgment. How different will they appear in the day of God from what they seem when we utter them.—*Review and Herald,* February 27, 1913 (*Messages to Young People,* 328).

Question 86:
Must we always kneel when we pray?

("Prayer Position")

I am wondering if you can help me by answering the following questions. In Ellen White's writings, are there details regarding the proper position for praying? Are there statements that support praying while standing up or sitting down?

Questions such as yours arise because Mrs. White said that kneeling is the "proper position always." But how do we understand that "always"? There are, indeed, statements from Mrs. White that speak approvingly of prayers offered in other positions, especially standing up. Is she contradicting herself?

I believe that a closer look will reveal there is no contradiction here at all. The situation Mrs. White was addressing when she insisted on kneeling was the congregational prayer before the sermon. Here is what she said.

> One who has been educated for about five years in Battle Creek was asked to lead in prayer before Sister White should speak to the people. But as I beheld him standing upright upon his feet while his lips were about to open in prayer to God, my soul was stirred within me to give him an open rebuke. Calling him by name, I said, "Get down upon your knees." This is the proper position always (*Selected Messages,* 2:311).

Let us not try to make Mrs. White's statement to one situation apply to all others. The "always" here, as I understand it, applies to the main prayer for the congregation during the worship service. It does not apply to other situations, as other statements she made indicate—situations such as "when you are walking, and when you are busy with your daily labor" (*The Ministry of Healing,* 511).

When we present the congregation before the One Mrs. White calls "the Sovereign of the universe," or for that matter, in our private prayers, the kneeling position properly represents our status as His subjects; it instills in us a sense of our own smallness and weakness, and it shows respect for One who is much greater than we and is "high and lifted up." It acknowledges our dependence on Him. What excuse do we have for not kneeling before Him in the church service when we come to present our petitions formally before Him? This, I believe, is the point Mrs. White was making. But other prayers, for other purposes and in other settings, may be offered in other positions. Thus, the Bible speaks, for instance, of Nehemiah offering a quick prayer for guidance while he stood before the king of Persia, who had asked him a question and was waiting for his reply. Such prayers are fine in Mrs. White's view.

Thus, the fact that Mrs. White allowed for other positions in prayer on other occasions does not, in my understanding, present a contradiction to her assertion that kneeling "is the proper position always" for one who is representing the congregation in the main prayer of the service.

Question 87:
Why did Elijah have to pray seven times?

("Elijah Statement")

About twenty or twenty-five years ago, I was reading a story about Elijah in a Spirit of Prophecy book and I came across something that made a deep impression on me. I have gone page by page through my books, but I have never been able to find it again. I finally came to the conclusion that I must not have read it at all, but then at church the other day, we had a video, and the pastor on the video quoted word for word what I had read so many years ago. Then he said that it was found in the Bible commentary. I don't have the Bible commentary, so I don't know how I ever read those words so long ago.

What really interested me in what I read was when Ellen White talked about Elijah kneeling seven times in prayer and that each time he knelt, he reviewed his life to see where he had failed to give God glory or bring God glory—something like that. Then the seventh time when he got up, there was that little cloud in the sky. I have read many stories about Elijah, but they didn't have the part where he reviewed his life. Could you see if that story is written that way in something that I have here at home?

Here is the statement you were looking for.

The servant watched while Elijah prayed. Six times he returned from the watch, saying, There is nothing, no cloud, no sign of rain. But the prophet did not give up in discouragement. He kept reviewing his life, to see where he had failed to honor God, he confessed his sins, and thus continued to afflict his soul before God, while watching for a token that his prayer was answered. As he searched his heart, he seemed to be less and less, both in his own estimation and in the sight of God. It seemed to him that he was nothing, and that God was everything; and when he reached the point of renouncing self, while he clung to the Saviour as his only strength and righteousness, the answer came. The servant appeared, and said, "Behold, there ariseth a little cloud out of the sea, like a man's hand" (*Review and Herald,* May 26, 1891; *The Seventh-day Adventist Bible Commentary,* 2:1035).

The statement also appears in a couple of devotional books: *Our Father Cares,* page 100, and *Our High Calling,* page 133. It was included as well in the compilation *Prayer,* page 140.

Yes, yes, and yes! That is the one I have tried to find for so many years. I love that part about Elijah searching his heart because that's where I am at right now. If Elijah, the prophet of God needed to search his heart and afflict his soul and review his life, how much more do I need to do that also! Jesus is coming soon!

Question 88:
Will only one in ten Adventists be saved?
(" 'Not One in Ten, in the Adventist Church, Would Be Saved' ")

Did Ellen White say that not one in ten in the Adventist Church will be saved? If so, where?

No, Mrs. White did not make such a statement. In the CD-ROM database, there is only one reference to "not one in ten," and that is addressing the question of how many ministers are suitably informed and competent to handle health questions. Mrs. White's more common expression was "not one in twenty." The closest we can come to what you asked for is this statement:

> It is a solemn statement that I make to the church, that not one in twenty whose names are registered upon the church books are prepared to close their earthly history, and would be as verily without God and without hope in the world as the common sinner. They are professedly serving God, but they are more earnestly serving mammon. This half-and-half work is a constant denying of Christ, rather than a confessing of Christ. So many have brought into the church their own unsubdued spirit, unrefined; their spiritual taste is perverted by their own immoral, debasing corruptions, symbolizing the world in spirit, in heart, in purpose, confirming themselves in lustful practices, and are full of deception through and through in their professed Christian life. Living as sinners, claiming to be Christians! Those who claim to be Christians and will confess Christ should come out from among them and touch not the unclean thing, and be separate (*Christian Service*, 41).

Though this is certainly a solemn statement, you can see that it is not a prediction of what will happen at the end but is a statement of conditions current at the time of the writing. The same may be said of her other statements of "not one in twenty" or "not one in a hundred." The outcome at the end will depend on the response of people to appeals such as those Mrs. White made and to the final events as they unfold.

We shouldn't take these statements literally, because never once does Ellen White write "not one in eight" or "not one in thirteen." She used the statements figuratively, to show the seriousness of the point she was making.

Question 89:
Do our angels leave us at the theater door?
("Angels Leave Us at the Theater or Bar?")

> *I remember as a child being told that Ellen White said we should not go into the theaters or bars because our guardian angels could not or would not go with us. I have tried to find this statement by looking in the index to her writings and by doing a search on your Web site. No success. I am beginning to think this is one of those "quotes" that isn't really there! Have you heard this statement before? If so, any idea where it can be found?*

I don't think there is a statement just like the ones you are asking about. Because I am usually asked about theaters rather than bars in this connection, I have gathered some statements that might be relevant to the theater issue, and I'll be glad to share them with you. The theater in her day, of course, was live theater, not movies. Its moral level, however, was probably as bad in its day as that of the movies today. Let me share with you several statements that may bear on the question you have asked about angels leaving us when we go to unsavory places.

> Angels of God will preserve His people while they walk in the path of duty, but there is no assurance of such protection for those who deliberately venture upon Satan's ground (*Testimonies for the Church*, 5:198).

The above statement doesn't deal with the theater, but it does indicate that by the choices we make, we can at least restrict, if not repulse, the work and even the presence of the angels. Surely this is a serious matter, not to be taken lightly.

Here is one statement that does refer to the theater in connection with angels:

> When about to accompany his wife and children to the theater or the ball-room, let the professed Christian ask himself, Can I seek God's blessing upon the scene of pleasure? Would my Master be a

guest at such a place? Will angels minister to me there? (*Signs of the Times,* February 23, 1882).

But note also this encouraging word:

The angels never leave the tempted ones a prey to the enemy, who would destroy the souls of men if permitted to do so. As long as there is hope, until they resist the Holy Spirit to their eternal ruin, men are guarded by heavenly intelligences (*Signs of the Times,* June 6, 1895).

See also question 31: What's wrong with going to the theater? And see question 32: What did Ellen White say about Christian drama?

Part 8

Miscellaneous Questions

Question 90:
How could Christ's deity not have died on the cross?
("Deity Did Not Die?")

> *Please give me some direction in a discussion I have been having regarding two Ellen G. White statements. The statements are as follows: "When Christ was crucified, it was His human nature that died. Deity did not sink and die; that would have been impossible" (Manuscript Releases, 21:418). " 'I am the resurrection, and the life' (John 11:25). He who had said, 'I lay down my life, that I might take it again' (John 10:17), came forth from the grave to life that was in Himself. Humanity died; divinity did not die. In His divinity, Christ possessed the power to break the bonds of death. He declares that He has life in Himself to quicken whom He will" (Selected Messages, 1:301).*
>
> *Could you refer me to some contemporary Adventist sources that comment on this concept of Christ's deity/divinity not dying? And please tell me whether the White Estate has any commentary on these statements.*

I don't know of contemporary Adventist sources that comment on this concept, though there may indeed be some. I think we are simply dealing with one of the mysteries of the Incarnation. Jesus was fully God and fully human, with His two natures blended into one. I found more of the statements you quoted in this reference from *The Seventh-day Adventist Bible Commentary,* (5:1113, 1114) in the "E. G. White Comments" on Mark 16:6:

6 (John 1:1-3, 14; Phil. 2:5-8; Col. 2:9; Heb. 1:6, 8; 2:14-17; Hebrews 4:15). Deity Did Not Die.—Was the human nature of the Son of Mary changed into the divine nature of the Son of God? No; the two natures were mysteriously blended in one person—the man Christ Jesus. In Him dwelt all the fullness of the Godhead bodily. When Christ was crucified, it was His human nature that died. Deity did not sink and die; that would have been impossible. Christ, the sinless One, will save every son and daughter of Adam who accepts the salvation proffered them, consenting to become the children of God. The Saviour has purchased the fallen race with His own blood.

This is a great mystery, a mystery that will not be fully, completely understood in all its greatness until the translation of the redeemed shall take place. Then the power and greatness and efficacy of the gift of God to man will be understood. But the enemy is determined that this gift shall be so mystified that it will become as nothingness (Letter 280, 1904). . . .

"I am the resurrection, and the life." He who had said, "I lay down my life, that I might take it again," came forth from the grave to life that was in Himself. Humanity died: divinity did not die. In His divinity, Christ possessed the power to break the bonds of death. He declares that He has life in Himself to quicken whom He will.

All created beings live by the will and power of God. They are recipients of the life of the Son of God. However able and talented, however large their capacities, they are replenished with life from the Source of all life. He is the spring, the fountain, of life. Only He who alone hath immortality, dwelling in light and life, could say, "I have power to lay down my life, and I have power to take it again." . . .

Christ was invested with the right to give immortality. The life which He had laid down in humanity, He again took up and gave to humanity. "I am come," He says, "that they might have life, and that they might have it more abundantly" (YI Aug. 4, 1898).

If God is by definition immortal, how can deity die? As Mrs. White said, "That would have been impossible." Yet Jesus died, and His death affected even His divinity. It did not die, but it was at least quiescent in the tomb. I don't understand all this, but I believe that something along this line must have happened. Perhaps this will be one of the themes of salvation that we will contemplate for eternity.

Question 91:
Will Jesus retain His human body forever?
("Jesus' Body Throughout Eternity")

I am wondering if Mrs. White said that Jesus would bear the human form throughout eternity and where she said it.

Probably the best-known statement that speaks to your question appears in *The Desire of Ages,* pages 25, 26:

By His life and His death, Christ has achieved even more than recovery from the ruin wrought through sin. It was Satan's purpose to bring about an eternal separation between God and man; but in Christ we become more closely united to God than if we had never fallen. In taking our nature, the Saviour has bound Himself to humanity by a tie that is never to be broken. Through the eternal ages He is linked with us. "God so loved the world, that He gave His only-begotten Son." John 3:16. He gave Him not only to bear our sins, and to die as our sacrifice; He gave Him to the fallen race. To assure us of His immutable counsel of peace, God gave His only-begotten Son to become one of the human family, forever to retain His human nature. This is the pledge that God will fulfill His word. "Unto *us* a child is born, unto *us* a son is given: and the government shall be upon His shoulder." God has adopted human nature in the person of His Son, and has carried the same into the highest heaven. It is the "Son of man" who shares the throne of the universe. It is the "Son of man" whose name shall be called, "Wonderful, Counselor, The mighty God, The everlasting Father, The Prince of Peace." Isa. 9:6. The I Am is the Daysman between God and humanity, laying His hand upon both. He who is "holy, harmless, undefiled, separate from sinners," is not ashamed to call us brethren. Heb. 7:26; 2:11. In Christ the family of earth and the family of heaven are bound together. Christ glorified is our brother. Heaven is enshrined in humanity, and humanity is enfolded in the bosom of Infinite Love.

Question 92:
Have people changed the words of our Bibles?
(" 'Changing the Words' ")

> *I would like you to explain what is meant by "learned men" changing "the words" in the following quoted excerpt. Is this talking about commentaries or other versions of the Bible?*

> *I saw that God had especially guarded the Bible; yet when copies of it were few, learned men had in some instances changed the words, thinking that they were making it more plain when in reality they were mystifying that which was plain, by causing it to lean to their established views, which were governed by tradition. But I saw that the Word of God, as a whole, is a perfect chain, one portion linking into and explaining another. True seekers for truth need not err; for not only is the Word of God plain and simple in declaring the way of life, but the Holy Spirit is given as a guide in understanding the way to life therein revealed (*Early Writings, 220, 221).*

I believe that when Mrs. White wrote of "learned men" having "in some instances changed the words, thinking that they were making it more plain," she wasn't thinking of newer translations of Scripture nor of commentaries. Rather, she was referring to the times when the only copies of the Bible were made by hand and therefore, they were few in comparison to what we have today.

In all, there are now several thousand manuscripts of portions (and occasionally all) of the New Testament, some dating back as far as the second century A.D., but most from the later centuries down to about the sixteenth century. No two of these manuscripts are just alike in every detail. There may be spelling differences, occasional mistakes of copying in which a word or a line is left out or repeated, and so forth. And then there are differences of wording. Many of the modern translations will tell you about these differences in the footnotes at the bottom of the page.

Mrs. White, I believe, was commenting on the tendency of some scribes, while copying, to make the text say what it "ought" to say—to "clarify" meanings that were obscure or troublesome to them, making the text conform to what they believed. Yet she expressed her confidence in our ability to find the truth in Scripture by comparing one part of Scripture with another, so that none need go astray. And in fact, the number of manuscripts we have for each portion of Scripture (so we can compare them) and the ways we have of evaluating the variations have given us even greater confidence that we have the text of the Bible as nearly as possible like it was written originally.

In another place, *Selected Messages,* 1:16, Mrs. White commented along a line similar to the passage you quoted.

> Some look to us gravely and say, "Don't you think there might have been some mistake in the copyist or in the translators?" This is all probable, and the mind that is so narrow that it will hesitate and stumble over this possibility or probability would be just as ready to stumble over the mysteries of the Inspired Word, because their feeble minds cannot see through the purposes of God. . . . All the mistakes will not cause trouble to one soul, or cause any feet to stumble, that would not manufacture difficulties from the plainest revealed truth.

Despite her recognition that such problems might have occurred, she had unbounded confidence in the Bible. She continued (on pages 17, 18),

> I take the Bible just as it is, as the Inspired Word. I believe its utterances in an entire Bible. Men arise who think they find something to criticize in God's Word. They lay it bare before others as evidence of superior wisdom. These men are, many of them, smart men, learned men, they have eloquence and talent, the whole lifework [of whom] is to unsettle minds in regard to the inspiration of the Scriptures. They influence many to see as they do. And the same work is passed on from one to another, just as Satan designed it should be, until we may see the full meaning of the words of Christ, "When the Son of man cometh, shall he find faith on the earth?" (Luke 18:8). . . .
>
> Brethren, cling to your Bible, as it reads, and stop your criticisms in regard to its validity, and obey the Word, and not one of you will be lost. . . .

Simplicity and plain utterance are comprehended by the illiterate, by the peasant, and the child as well as by the full-grown man or the giant in intellect. If the individual is possessed of large talents of mental powers, he will find in the oracles of God treasures of truth, beautiful and valuable, which he can appropriate. He will also find difficulties, and secrets and wonders which will give him the highest satisfaction to study during a long lifetime, and yet there is an infinity beyond.

As for modern translations and commentaries, Mrs. White herself used them. You will find a number of quotations from versions of the Bible other than the King James Version in many of her later works, when these other versions were available. She also consulted Bible commentaries occasionally. So I believe that these are not what she was referring to in *Early Writings*.

Question 93:
Are the modern Bible translations dangerous?
("New Bible Versions")

> *Can you advise me on any writings of Ellen G. White that make refer-*
> *ence to new versions of the Bible being printed in these days to disseminate*
> *falsehoods?*

I know of no statement from Mrs. White warning against new versions of the Bible that would be produced to spread falsehoods. We have a document regarding Mrs. White's own use of different versions of Scripture. It reveals something of her attitude toward a variety of Bible translations:

> In her writings Ellen White made use of the various English trans-
> lations of the Holy Scriptures that were available in her day. She does
> not, however, comment directly on the relative merits of these ver-
> sions, but it is clear from her practice that she recognized the desir-
> ability of making use of the best in all versions of the Bible. What she
> has written lays a broad foundation for an open-minded approach to
> the many renderings of the Sacred Text. . . .
>
> On Mrs. White's attitude toward the English revision of the 1880s,
> her son, W. C. White, reports:

> > "Before the revised version was published, there
> > leaked out from the committee statements regarding
> > changes which they intended to make. Some of these
> > I brought to Mother's attention, and she gave me
> > very surprising information regarding these Scrip-
> > tures. This led me to believe that the revision, when
> > it came to hand, would be a matter of great service to
> > us."—W. C. White, DF 579 (1931); *Ministry*, April,
> > 1947, p. 17.

It is significant that almost immediately after the appearance of the English Revised Version, Mrs. White made use of it in her books, as she did also of the American Standard Revision when it became available in 1901. . . .

As to Mrs. White's attitude toward the revisions of 1885 and 1901, and as to her own use of these in preaching and writing, her son, W. C. White, who was closely associated with her in her public ministry and in the preparation and publication of her books, wrote in 1931:

> "I do not know of anything in the E. G. White writings, nor can I remember of anything in Sister White's conversations, that would intimate that she felt that there was any evil in the use of the Revised Version. . . .
>
> "As manuscripts were prepared for her new books and for revised editions of books already in print, Sister White's attention was called from time to time by myself and Sister Marian Davis, to the fact that she was using texts which were much more clearly translated in the Revised Version. Sister White studied each one carefully, and in some cases she instructed us to use the Revised Version. In other cases she instructed us to adhere to the Authorized Version [King James Version].
>
> "When *Testimonies for the Church,* vol. 8, was printed and it seemed desirable to make some lengthy quotations from the Psalms, it was pointed out to Sister White that the Revised Version of these Psalms was preferable, and that by using the form of blank verse the passages were more readable. Sister White gave the matter deliberate consideration, and instructed us to use the Revised Version" (Arthur L. White, "The E. G. White Counsel on Versions of the Bible").

Question 94:
Did Ellen White say anything about dinosaurs?
("Dinosaurs")

> *Please provide me with any references Sister White might have made concerning dinosaurs and whether they were taken on Noah's ark.*

Ellen White did not mention dinosaurs by name. Many people, though, think she was referring to them in statements such as the following, from the *Spiritual Gifts* volumes. If this is correct, the first one answers your question about whether they were on the ark:

> Every species of animal which God had created were preserved in the ark. The confused species which God did not create, which were the result of amalgamation, were destroyed by the flood (*Spiritual Gifts*, 3:75).

> Bones of men and animals are found in the earth, in mountains and in valleys, showing that much larger men and beasts once lived upon the earth. I was shown that very large, powerful animals existed before the flood which do not now exist. Instruments of warfare are sometimes found; also petrified wood. Because the bones of human beings and of animals found in the earth, are much larger than those of men and animals now living, or that have existed for many generations past, some conclude that the world is older than we have any scriptural record of, and was populated long before the record of creation, by a race of beings vastly superior in size to men now upon the earth (*Spiritual Gifts*, 3:92, 93).

> There were a class of very large animals which perished at the flood. God knew that the strength of man would decrease, and these mammoth animals could not be controlled by feeble man (*Spiritual Gifts*, 4a:121).

The first statement indicates that the "confused species which God did not create" were the result of "amalgamation," and they were not preserved in the ark but perished in the Flood. Mrs. White did not spell out how this amalgamation came about. Attempts to define it more precisely are of necessity just speculation. I do not know whether or not human beings had a part in that. Mrs. White simply does not say.

See also the following question and answer.

Question 95:
What does Ellen White's statement about amalgamation mean?
("Amalgamation and Black People")

> *A few years back, an article came out in the* Adventist Review *that was quite shocking regarding something Ellen White had said. I am wondering if you can find where she made the statement. The* Review *article said that she said black people came from the sexual union of a white person with an animal. (I think it might have said an ape.)*

Back in January of 1995, a *Review* author answered a question from a reader who said that Mrs. White had claimed a fruitful mating of humans and animals. Perhaps this is the item you remember reading. To put the answer in a few words, the claim that Mrs. White said this is simply not true—she did not say that.

The following is from pages 491, 492 of *Messenger of the Lord,* an informative and helpful book by Herbert E. Douglass.

> Critics have charged that Ellen White wrote in 1864 (and republished in 1870) that humans once cohabited with animals and that their offspring produced certain races that exist today. [Ellen White's] statement reads: "But if there was one sin above another which called for the destruction of the race by the flood, it was the base crime of amalgamation of man and beast which defaced the image of God, and caused confusion everywhere. God purposed to destroy by a flood that powerful, long-lived race that had corrupted their ways before Him" [*Spiritual Gifts,* 3:64].
>
> No dictionary has ever used "amalgamation" to describe the cohabitation of man with beast. . . . Nineteenth-century usage included the mixing of diverse races. . . .
>
> On two other occasions, Mrs. White used the word "amalgamation." She used it metaphorically, comparing faithful believers and worldlings. [Note: "Those who profess to be followers of Christ, should be living agencies, cooperating with heavenly intelligences; but by union with the world, the character of God's people becomes tar-

nished, and through amalgamation with the corrupt, the fine gold becomes dim" (*Review and Herald,* August 23, 1892).] And she used it to describe the origin of poisonous plants and other irregularities in the biological world: " . . . Every noxious herb is of [Satan's] sowing, and by his ingenious methods of amalgamation he has corrupted the earth with tares" [*Selected Messages,* 2:288].

Recognizing that Satan has been an active agent in the corrupting of God's plan for man, beast, plants, etc., we can better understand what Ellen White may have meant when she described the results of amalgamation. That which "defaced the image of God" in man and that which "confused the species [of animals]" has been the handi-work of Satan with the cooperation of humans. Such "amalgamation of man and [of] beast, as may be seen in the almost endless varieties of species of animals, and in certain races of men," becomes understand-able.

Mrs. White never hinted of subhuman beings or any kind of hy-brid animal-human relationship. She did speak of "species of animals" and "races of men" but not any kind of amalgam of animals with hu-man beings.

Here is the key statement that I think helps us to determine what Mrs. White did mean, or at least what she did not mean: "Every species of animal which God had created were preserved in the ark. The confused species which God did not create, which were the result of amalgamation, were destroyed by the flood. Since the flood there has been amalgamation of man and beast, as may be seen in the almost endless varieties of species of animals, and in certain races of men" (*Spiritual Gifts,* 3:75).

The question is whether "amalgamation of man and beast" here means amalgamation of human beings *with* beasts or amalgamation of human beings with human beings and of beasts with beasts. Though I am not entirely sure what Mrs. White had in mind in this statement (which she dropped from later reworkings of this material), I have to conclude that she had the latter interpretation in view, since this amalgamation, she said, has brought about "the almost endless varieties of species of animals."

Think about it. Did the great variety of animals result from a union of human being with beast? No one I know of argues that this great variety is due to any such "amalgamation," nor have I heard anyone try to claim that Mrs. White believed that of the animals. Her critics always focus on the narrower question of some midway species, part human and part beast, and often they try to say that her reference to "certain races of men" indicates that she considered blacks to be a result of such a crossing. I don't believe it. What she actually did say in this paragraph is incompatible, in my opinion, with the idea that offspring were formed by a union of humans and animals. Note that in the last sentence of the statement she clearly distinguished man from beast even after the amalgamation had taken place. Where would be the dividing line if the two had crossed? Further, Ellen White made no connection between this amalgamation and blacks.

It is much easier to say what I believe Mrs. White did *not* mean than it is to show what she did mean. If she did not intend to convey the idea of amalgamation of human beings *with* beasts, then she must have meant amalgamation of human being with human being and of beast with beast, the results of which, she said, could still be seen in the great variety in the animal kingdom and in certain races of men.

As for amalgamation among humans and what Mrs. White may have meant by that, we don't have much to go on there either. The closest I know of in Mrs. White's writings is her explanation of Genesis 6:2, 4, in *Patriarchs and Prophets,* pages 81, 82. There she says when " 'the sons of God [Seth's descendants] saw the daughters of men [Cain's descendants] that they were fair' " and intermarried with them, "sin spread abroad in the earth like a deadly leprosy."

Did Mrs. White have this kind of crossing in mind in her amalgamation statement? I don't know. This interpretation does have the virtue of parallel citing: where the Bible gives the mixing of the "sons of God" with the "daughters of men" as a cause leading up to the Flood, Mrs. White similarly lists amalgamation as such a cause. Was she implying that these were the same transgression? I don't think we can determine this well enough to satisfy everyone.

See also the preceding question and answer.

Question 96:
Should people of other races not seek equality with white people?
("Ellen G. White Statements Race")

> *On page 214 of volume 9 of the* Testimonies, *there is a sentence that is puzzling to me in light of many other statements. It is the first sentence of the third paragraph: "The colored people should not urge that they be placed on an equality with white people." But Mrs. White says over and over that we all stand equal before God.*

If removed from its context, this statement may appear to say that Ellen White did not consider "colored people" to be equal to whites. However, other statements reveal explicitly that she did consider all equal, and this statement in its context shows that her concern was evangelistic, not discriminatory. Notice these statements about equality:

> No distinction on account of nationality, race, or caste, is recognized by God. He is the Maker of all mankind. All men are of one family by creation, and all are one through redemption (*Christ's Object Lessons*, 386).

> The black man's name is written in the book of life beside the white man's. All are one in Christ. Birth, station, nationality, or color cannot elevate or degrade men (*Selected Messages*, 2:343).

Now, note the context of evangelism that immediately follows the statement you quoted.

> The relation of the two races has been a matter hard to deal with, and I fear that it will ever remain a most perplexing problem. So far as possible, everything that would stir up the race prejudice of the white people should be avoided. There is danger of closing the door so that our white laborers will not be able to work in some places in the South.
> I know that if we attempt to meet the ideas and preferences of

some of the colored people, we shall find our way blocked completely. The work of proclaiming the truth for this time is not to be hindered by an effort to adjust the position of the Negro race. Should we attempt to do this we should find that barriers like mountains would be raised to hinder the work that God desires to have done. If we move quietly and judiciously, laboring in the way that God has marked out, both white and colored people will be benefited by our labors.

The time has not come for us to work as if there were no prejudice. Christ said: "Be ye therefore wise as serpents, and harmless as doves." Matthew 10:16. If you see that by doing certain things which you have a perfect right to do, you hinder the advancement of God's work, refrain from doing those things. Do nothing that will close the minds of others against the truth. There is a world to save, and we shall gain nothing by cutting loose from those we are trying to help. All things may be lawful, but all things are not expedient.

The wise course is the best. As laborers together with God, we are to work in the way that will enable us to accomplish the most for Him. Let none go to extremes. We need wisdom from above; for we have a difficult problem to solve. If rash moves are made now, great mischief will be done. The matter is to be presented in such a way that the truly converted colored people will cling to the truth for Christ's sake, refusing to renounce one principle of sound Bible doctrine because they may think that the very best course is not being pursued toward the Negro race (*Testimonies for the Church*, 9:214, 215; see also 208, 209).

I think statements like these make clear Mrs. White's position on the matter. She hoped for a better day, in which such prejudices would not dominate, and by God's grace I think we have come to such a day. But until that could happen, it was still necessary for the gospel message to go forward, and she called on believers to be wise in these matters in order to allow the message to be heard.

See also the following question and answer.

Question 97:
Did Ellen White say the genes of all the races were in Adam?
("Origin of Colored Races")

> *A friend of mine said she had read somewhere in an E. G. White book that the genes of all the colored races were in Adam. However, she can't remember exactly where she read that. Is there such a statement?*

I know of no statement from Mrs. White that makes the point you have asked about. It is a striking statement, isn't it? That very fact makes me think that if it had genuinely come from Mrs. White, it would be quite well known.

But even if Mrs. White didn't make a statement about the genes of the various races all being in Adam, she clearly upheld the full brotherhood of all mankind.

Christ came to this earth with a message of mercy and forgiveness. He laid the foundation for a religion by which Jew and Gentile, black and white, free and bond, are linked together in one common brotherhood, recognized as equal in the sight of God (*Testimonies,* 7:225).

No distinction on account of nationality, race, or caste, is recognized by God. He is the Maker of all mankind. All men are of one family by creation, and all are one through redemption. Christ came to demolish every wall of partition, to throw open every compartment of the temple, that every soul may have free access to God. . . . In Christ there is neither Jew nor Greek, bond nor free. All are brought nigh by His precious blood (*Christ's Object Lessons,* 386).

The religion of the Bible recognizes no caste or color. It ignores rank, wealth, worldly honor. God estimates men as men. With Him, character decides their worth. And we are to recognize the Spirit of Christ in whomsoever it is revealed (*Testimonies,* 9:223).

The walls of sectarianism and caste and race will fall down when the true missionary spirit enters the hearts of men. Prejudice is melted away by the love of God (*Review and Herald,* Jan. 21, 1896; *The Southern Work,* 1966 ed., 55).

Walls of separation have been built up between the whites and the blacks. These walls of prejudice will tumble down of themselves as did the walls of Jericho, when Christians obey the Word of God, which enjoins on them supreme love to their Maker and impartial love to their neighbors (*Review and Herald,* December 17, 1895; republished in *The Southern Work,* 1966 ed., 43).

When the Holy Spirit moves upon human minds, all petty complaints and accusations between man and his fellow man will be put away. . . . In our worship of God there will be no distinction between rich and poor, white and black. All prejudice will be melted away. When we approach God, it will be as one brotherhood (*Review and Herald,* Oct. 24, 1899, 677).

The Lord's eye is upon all His creatures; He loves them all, and makes no difference between white and black, except that He has a special, tender pity for those who are called to bear a greater burden than others. . . .

Whoever of the human family give themselves to Christ, whoever hear the truth and obey it, become children of one family. The ignorant and the wise, the rich and the poor, the heathen and the slave, white or black—Jesus paid the purchase money for their souls. If they believe on Him, His cleansing blood is applied to them. The black man's name is written in the book of life beside the white man's. All are one in Christ. Birth, station, nationality, or color cannot elevate or degrade men. The character makes the man. If a red man, a Chinese, or an African gives his heart to God, in obedience and faith, Jesus loves him none the less for his color. He calls him His well-beloved brother. . . .

Men may have both hereditary and cultivated prejudices, but when the love of Jesus fills the heart, and they become one with Christ, they will have the same spirit that He had. If a colored brother sits by their side, they will not be offended or despise him. They are journeying to the same heaven, and will be seated at the same table to eat bread in the kingdom of God. If Jesus is abiding in our hearts we cannot despise the colored man who has the same Saviour abiding in his heart (Published in *The Southern Work,* 1966 ed., 12–14).

See also the preceding question and answer.

Question 98:
Was Ellen White of mixed-race ancestry?
("Ellen G. White's Background/Ethnicity")

> *I was having a discussion with some friends about Mrs. White's writings, and one man said, "Did you know that Mrs. White was of mixed ethnicity?" Some others said sure, she was both white and black, and many in the group agreed. I had never heard this before, so I am curious, and I figured if anyone would know, it would be someone at the White Estate. Is this true, and if so, is there historical documentation?*

The question you have asked has been around for a long time, principally, I think, because certain pictures of Ellen G. White portray her with features that resemble those of people of African descent. And, indeed, at some point such a background may be shown to be true for her. But for now, no one has been able to demonstrate an African or Native American component to her ancestry.

Elder Charles Dudley has been working diligently on this. He finds people of mixed heritage who bear various versions of the name *Gould* (Ellen White's mother's maiden name, and Ellen White's middle name) living in Delaware, New Jersey, and some other places, if I recall correctly. But he hasn't been able to demonstrate a blood link from Mrs. White to them. Though he remains convinced that these are Ellen G. White's "cousins," the genealogical tie has yet to be demonstrated.

For a report on the latest research and for the White Estate's conclusion, see the statement titled "The Genealogy of Ellen G. White—an Update," available on the Ellen G. White Estate Web site.

Question 99:
What was Ellen White's favorite hymn?
("Favorite Hymn Question")

I was wondering whether you know if there was a hymn that Ellen White especially liked.

According to Ella White Robinson, one of Mrs. White's older grandchildren who knew her well, Mrs. White declared her favorite hymn to be "Jesus, Lover of My Soul." Beyond that, she had many hymns that she loved, not all of which are well known today. Among these are "There Is Sunlight on the Hilltop," "O Worship the King," "Holy, Holy, Holy," "All Hail the Power of Jesus' Name," "Just As I Am," "I Will Follow Thee, My Savior," "Is My Name Written There?" "I'm a Pilgrim," "I Will Never, Never Leave Thee," "We Speak of the Realms of the Blest," and "There Are Angels Hov'ring Round." In the White home, as the boys were growing up, each morning when they gathered for worship they sang, "Lord, in the Morning," and in the evening they sang, "Sweet Hour of Prayer."

Question 100:
Could Lucifer sing four parts simultaneously?
("Music—Could Satan Carry Four Parts?")

Could Satan carry four parts at the same time—producing four-part harmony?

From a letter written by Arthur L. White,

"You ask if we can help you find a statement that you are of the opinion you have read somewhere saying that Lucifer could sing four parts at one time. I do not know where you may have read this statement. Some others have made inquiry of us on this same point. However, we have never been able to find such a statement in Mrs. White's writings, published or unpublished. I am sorry for the disappointment that this word will bring you, but this is the situation."

Question 101: **Did John the Baptist eat bugs?**

("Question on the Locust John the Baptist Ate")

> *Kindly advise me on what type of locusts John the Baptist ate. Some people say that the locusts mentioned are insects, while others say there were wild fruits called locusts.*

The truth is that neither English translations of the passage nor the Greek in which the New Testament was originally written tells us clearly what John ate. While the Greek word favors the insect, there is a substantial body of evidence from the ancient world that favors the carob pod. *The Seventh-day Adventist Bible Commentary* has quite an extensive discussion of this in volume 5, note 1, in "Additional Notes on Chapter 3" on Matthew 3.

Mrs. White makes the following comment about John the Baptist in *Testimonies for the Church*, volume 3, page 62: "John separated himself from friends and from the luxuries of life. . . . His diet, purely vegetable, of locusts and wild honey, was a rebuke to the indulgence of appetite and the gluttony that everywhere prevailed."

Bibliography

Ellen G. White Books[1]

The Acts of the Apostles (AA). Mountain View, Calif.: Pacific Press® Publishing Association, 1911.

The Adventist Home (AH). Nashville, Tenn.: Southern Publishing Association, 1952.

Child Guidance (CG). Nashville, Tenn.: Southern Publishing Association, 1954.

Christian Service, Instruction for Effective (CS). Washington, D.C.: Review and Herald® Publishing Association, 1947.

Christ's Object Lessons (COL). Washington, D.C.: Review and Herald®, 1941.

Colporteur Ministry (CM). Mountain View, Calif.: Pacific Press®, 1953.

Counsels on Diet and Foods (CD). Washington, D.C.: Review and Herald®, 1938.

Counsels on Health and Instruction to Medical Missionary Workers. (CH). Mountain View, Calif.: Pacific Press®, 1951.

The Desire of Ages (DA). Mountain View, Calif.: Pacific Press®, 1940.

Early Writings (EW). Washington, D.C.: Review and Herald®, 1945.

Evangelism (Ev). Washington, D.C.: Review and Herald®, 1946.

---

1. The letters in parentheses are the commonly accepted abbreviations for these books and periodicals. In the case of multivolume books, the volume number usually precedes the abbreviation with the page number following it (1SM 234), but sometimes the volume number joins the page number and follows the abbreviation (SM 1:234).

Gospel Workers (GW). Washington, D.C.: Review and Herald®, 1915.

The Great Controversy Between Christ and Satan (GC). Mountain View, Calif.: Pacific Press®, 1950.

In Heavenly Places (HP). Hagerstown, Md.: Review and Herald®, 1995.

Last Day Events (LDE). Boise, Idaho: Pacific Press®, 1992.

Life Sketches of Ellen G. White (LS). Mountain View, Calif.: Pacific Press®, 1943.

Manuscript Releases. (1MR) 21 vols. Silver Spring, Md.: Ellen G. White Estate, 1981–1993.

Messages to Young People (MYP). Nashville: Southern Publishing Association, 1930.

The Ministry of Healing (MH). Mountain View, Calif.: Pacific Press®, 1942.

Our Father Cares. Hagerstown, Md.: Review and Herald®, 1991.

Our High Calling (OHC). Washington, D.C.: Review and Herald®, 1961.

Patriarchs and Prophets (PP). Mountain View, Calif.: Pacific Press®, 1958.

Prayer. Nampa, Idaho: Pacific Press®, 2002.

Prophets and Kings (PK). Mountain View, Calif.: Pacific Press®, 1943.

The Retirement Years,. Hagerstown, Md.: Review and Herald®, 1990.

Selected Messages (1SM). 3 vols. Washington, D.C.: Review and Herald®, 1958–1980.

Sketches From the Life of Paul. Washington, D.C.: Review and Herald®, 1974.

The Southern Work (SW). Washington, D.C.: Review and Herald®, 1966.

Special Testimonies, Series A and B. Payson, Ariz.: Leaves-of-Autumn Books, c1904.

Spirit of Prophecy. (1SP). 4 vols. Mountain View, Calif.: Pacific Press®, 1870–1884.

Spiritual Gifts (1SG). 4 vols. Washington, D.C.: Review and Herald®, 1944–1945.

Steps to Christ (SC). Washington, D.C.: Review and Herald®, 1956.

Testimonies for the Church (1T). 9 vols. Mountain View, Calif.: Pacific Press®, 1948.

Testimonies on Sexual Behavior, Adultery, and Divorce (TSB). Silver Spring, Md.: Ellen G. White Estate, 1989.

Testimonies to Ministers and Gospel Workers (TM). Mountain View, Calif.: Pacific Press®, 1944.

Thoughts From the Mount of Blessing (MB). Mountain View, Calif.: Pacific Press®, 1956.

Ellen G. White Periodical References

The Advent Review and Sabbath Herald; Review and Herald (RH).

The Bible Echo and Signs of the Times (BEcho).

General Conference Bulletin (GCB).

The Home Missionary (HM).

Signs of the Times (ST).

The Youth's Instructor (YI).

Other Books

Douglass, Herbert E. *Messenger of the Lord.* Nampa, Idaho: Pacific Press®, 1998.

Ellen G. White Board of Trustees. *Comprehensive Index to the Writings of Ellen G. White.* 3 vols. Mountain View, Calif.: Pacific Press®, 1962.

Loughborough, J. N. *The Great Second Advent Movement: Its Rise and Progress.* Nashville: Southern Publishing Association, 1905.

Ministerial Association of the General Conference of Seventh-day Adventists. *The Seventh-day Adventist Ministers Handbook.* Silver Spring, Md.: General Conference of Seventh-day Adventists, 1997.

Nichol, Francis D., ed. *The Seventh-day Adventist Bible Commentary.* (1BC) 7 vols. Washington, D.C.: Review and Herald®, 1980.

Olson, A. V. *Thirteen Crisis Years: 1888–1901.* Washington, D.C.: Review and Herald®, 1981.

Secretariat, General Conference of Seventh-day Adventists. *Seventh-day Adventist Church Manual.* Hagerstown, Md.: Review and Herald®, 2005.

White, Arthur L. *Ellen G. White.* 6 vols. Washington, D.C.: Review and Herald®, 1981–1986.

White, James. *A Word to the Little Flock.* A facsimile edition with foreword by the Trustees of the Ellen G. White Publications. Washington, D.C.: Review and Herald®, n.d. (Available at http://drc.whiteestate.org/files/1322.pdf.)

Other Periodicals

Adventist Review.

Ministry.